The Popular Training Series From
Practical Horseman

Lessons
with
Lendon

25 progressive dressage lessons
take you from basic "whoa and go"
to your first competition.

By Lendon Gray
Produced by the Editors of
Practical Horseman Magazine

LESSONS WITH LENDON

By Lendon Gray and the Editors of Practical Horseman

Printed in the USA.

First Published in 2003 by PRIMEDIA Equine Network
656 Quince Orchard Road, #600
Gaithersburg, MD 20878
301-977-3900

VP, Group Publishing Director: Susan Harding
Director, Product Marketing: Julie Beaulieu
Editorial Director: Cathy Laws

Order by calling 800-957-5813 or online at www.TheEquineCollection.com

Practical Horseman
PO Box 589, Unionville, PA 19375
Editor: Mandy Lorraine
Editor-at-large: Kip Goldreyer
Articles Editor: Deborah Lyons
Editorial / Production Coordinator: Susan E. Simone
Photographer: Mandy Lorraine

Book Design: Lauryl Suire Eddlemon

Library of Congress Cataloging-in-Publication Data

Gray, Lendon.
  Lessons with Lendon : 25 progressive dressage lessons take you from
basic "whoa and go" to your first competition / by Lendon Gray.
    p. cm.
  ISBN 1-929164-16-5
  1. Dressage. I. Title.
  SF309.5 .G728 2003
  798.2'3--dc22
                                        2003018958

Contents

Special thanks to the following riders for their assistance with this series:

Erin Collins, Kerrie March, Marjaleena Ihalainen Berger, Brandilee Hilbert,
Courtney King, Michele Babkine, and Erica Hogg

---

*And to these horses and their owners, without whom
this book could not have been produced:*

Regal, owned by Erin Collins

Aastrakhan, owned by Wendy Luscombe

Cody, owned by Kathleen Tow

Ghirahdelli, owned by Maura Paulekas

Idocus, owned by Chris McCarthy

Scenic, Jamboree and Tab, owned by Lendon Gray

Lucas, owned by Albert Zesiger

Tucker, owned by Denise Lee

Umego, owned by Joni Cherbo

Wonderland, owned by Joni Cherbo

Sancho Panza, owned by Jeanne Pacchiana

Lindekrona, owned by Sam Grunkorn

Ravel, owned by Francine Walker

Toddingham, owned by Leslie Hargreaves

L.A. Baltic Sunstorm, owned by Janet Bell

Six Pack To Go, owned by Nancy Roper

Joseph, owned by Jennifer Benson

Introduction

HI, THERE! WELCOME! AND THANKS for joining me!

As anybody who's ever studied or worked with me knows, I believe that dressage is a discipline for every rider and every horse. Everybody can do it, and everybody can benefit from it. This book, based on the "Lesson With Lendon" series of columns I created in cooperation with *Practical Horseman* magazine, springs from that belief—and offers you an invitation to share in that belief of mine and find out what it can do for you and *your* horse.

You say you can walk, trot, and canter pretty comfortably, but you've never tried dressage (though maybe you've thought about it)? Or you're just getting interested in it? Or maybe you've been doing it for a while but would like a simpler, more down-to-earth approach to building your skills than the one you've gotten in the lessons you've had? Or, like several trail-riding students I teach, maybe you're involved in a completely different aspect of our sport and simply want to develop tools to improve your horse's ridability. Whatever your reasons, this book—like dressage!—is for you!

What IS Dressage?

Dressage (the word actually just means "training") is *communication*. With dressage, you develop a vocabulary that helps you talk to your horse in terms he can under-stand, so you get his cooperation. The longer you do dressage, the bigger your vocabulary. Eventually you can ask him to do anything—go fast, go slow, put his head up, put his head down, straighten, go crooked, shorten his body, lengthen, piaffe, gallop down a hill, or make a quick roll-back turn in the jumping field. Along the way, dressage will help your horse become the best he can be. Even if he's never fabu-lous, he'll be more ridable, more comfort-able, more athletic, and—I promise—better than he is now.

In each of this book's twenty-seven "Lessons," we'll take a simple, bite-sized piece of dressage and explore it with step-by-step instructions and pictures. I'm not kidding about keeping things simple: You can't change everything at once, and noth-ing is more frustrating than "sort of" work-ing on ten things simultaneously. So we'll focus on one thing and fix it. If the first way I give you doesn't work, I'll have another one that will. And in many of the Lessons you'll find one or two examples of what I'm calling "Lendon's Challenge": a simple, clear checkpoint to help you test your progress.

Some of the bite-sized pieces we'll focus on—holding your left hand too low, letting your heel come up, jerking on the right rein—are things you can fix right away. Others—feel, half-halts, sitting trot—you'll continue to explore for the rest of your life. Dressage is, above all, a long-term project. To put it all in perspective, I urge you (as I urge all my students) to write down your goals for your lifetime, this year, this month, this week, even today. Every so often, update the list. I think you'll be pleasantly surprised to see how often you accomplish in six months something you thought would take forever, and I know you'll have fun adding new goals as you attain the old ones.

And speaking of goals . . .

Most of us reach the point eventually where we want to show—and the last few chapters of this book will give you the tools you'd need to go to and enjoy your first Training Level show. There's also an "appendix" chapter, "Show Preparation," that'll give you a month-by-month breakdown, starting five months out, of things you'll want to do to be ready for your show.

I'll Do My Part; You Do Yours

As I see it, this book is a partnership. You're going to have fun, and I'll help you do so, but you'll have to kick in your share: self-discipline, consistency, and commitment. So indulge me for a moment while I climb onto my soapbox (something you'll see me continue to do from time to time).

Dressage isn't complicated. You don't need an enormous amount of talent to do it. Your horse doesn't have to be brilliant. And you can get by with spending an amazingly small amount of time in the saddle. But you *do* have to dedicate yourself, from the moment you get on your horse's back to the moment you get off, to giving him one hundred percent of your attention, shutting out distractions such as the fight you had with your boyfriend or what

you're going to cook for supper.

Here's why: In Lesson 1, for example, I'm going to tell you, "No more bangedy, bangedy, bangedy with your leg. Your horse is supposed to go when you touch him." So you tell *him*, "You are going to go to my leg, horse. I ask nicely, you don't go, I give you a kick or a touch with the whip and say 'LISTEN, YOU—GO TO MY LEG!'" But suppose that five minutes later, or tomorrow, or next week, when you're not so focused, you go back to bangedy-banging. Suddenly you remember, "Oh wait! Lendon said you're supposed to go to my leg." You put your leg on, he doesn't answer (naturally), so you kick him or smack him. That's not fair. It's almost abuse, and abuse never teaches a horse anything good. It just blows his mind or makes him duller and duller until he tunes you out completely.

The good news is that you can develop discipline and consistency the way you develop quiet hands or a good seat—with practice. School for as long as you can maintain your focus, even if it's only five minutes. Then walk on a long rein or go for a trail ride. Tomorrow, try to increase the time to ten minutes. And don't think discipline means you have to pound away at schooling every day. If you can only focus 100 percent for one day a week, school one day. In the long run, you'll achieve more than if you ride every day but focus less than 90 percent on days 2 through 7. Believe me, focusing any less than 90 percent isn't good enough. It'll even undo what you accomplished on day 1.

Finally, be realistic. If discipline and commitment aren't your cup of tea, you and your horse may be better off trail-riding. I have no argument with that. It's never wrong to have fun and enjoy your horse. It's only wrong to treat him unfairly.

The One Thing I Can't Do

I'll help you do a lot to change your horse's way of going as we work through these lessons. But I can't change his basic personality, because a horse's nature is his nature. When Last Scene, my incredibly wonderful little Grand Prix horse, came to me, he had boundless nervous energy. All he would do was run at a hundred miles an hour, like a hackney pony. As the months went by, I wanted to tear my hair out. I thought I was getting nowhere—teaching him "whoa" took a whole year. But I had to stay patient and never lose my temper. It was his nature to be hot. If I'd let myself get angry, grabbed his mouth, and set him in a frame, I could have gotten him to give me stuff, but never what he gave me in the end. I plugged away, kept my cool (writing down my goals for him sure came in handy!), and over time I was able to help him pour his energy into work. Moral: If you don't think you have the patience to deal with your horse's nature—be it jittery and sensitive or bone-lazy—maybe he's not the horse for you.

Now, let's get down to business.

About the Author

Generous, outspoken, pragmatic—that's two-time Olympian Lendon Gray, who makes no secret of her conviction that dressage is for EVERY horse and rider. The students she teaches range from kids and adult-amateurs just learning to post to those riding at international levels; their horses range from Morgans and Arabians through Quarter Horses and Appaloosas to Thoroughbreds and European warmbloods—as well as a goodly sprinkling of "just horses."

"People say, 'Why do you teach beginners? It's a waste of your talent.' But teaching beginners is a tremendous challenge. Training upper-level riders on fancy horses isn't that difficult. The challenge lies in taking those who aren't so experienced or talented and helping them get better on horses that weren't particularly born for dressage."

A Maine native who did much of her dressage work with fellow Down Easter Michael Poulin, Lendon was a member of the US Equestrian Team Olympic squad in 1980 (the "alternate Olympics," whose riding component took place in France) and 1988 (Seoul). She's also won nearly thirty National Championships—more than any other rider.

These days, when she's not teaching and training at her Bedford, New York, barn, Lendon is likely to be traveling the country giving clinics and judging. Or she might be preparing for, running, or sorting out the results of the Northeast Junior/Young Riders Dressage Championship Show, which she started in 1999 and which—with its equitation, dressage, and written test components; top judges; and equal-opportunity/can-do attitude—has become a prime draw for young dressageniks and their coaches.

LENDON'S CHALLENGE

Stay in two-point, balanced over your leg and not gripping with your knee or tightening your back, while you walk, trot, canter, lengthen stride, and do downward transitions to develop your position without interfering with your horse. That's what Courtney is doing here: seat out of the saddle, weight in her heel, "shock absorbers" (ankle, knee, and hip angles) working to stay with Umego's trot, hand independent of the neck, straight line from elbow to bit, and a nice loop in the reins.

LESSON 1

Can You "Do Nothing"?

EVERY TIME I GIVE A CLINIC, somebody asks me, "How do I get my horse's head down?" I always answer, "Before you can ask anything of him, you have to make sure that you speak with your aids only when you mean to, and that you can go with him without interfering."

When you hang on the reins or clutch your horse's sides, *you* become a second girth. You "use up your aids," so you don't have anything left to talk with. When you kick, kick, kick, and go left-right, left-right, seesaw, seesaw, wiggle, wiggle, wiggle, you fill the communication space between the two of you with non-stop, deafening, ineffective chatter. You can't expect him to respond, and you certainly can't hope for anything like self-carriage, because you never allow him to give it to you—you're always *asking*.

In this lesson, I'll help you go with your horse, without interfering—I call it "being invisible to your horse." I'll show you first how to fix your basic position, then how to secure it, then how to make him go on his own. You'll need only simple equipment: a snaffle that fits, a dressage whip to reinforce your leg aids, gloves, an ASTM/SEI-approved helmet, boots with a heel, and any kind of saddle (as long as it fits and is balanced).

How about your bit? In theory, every horse should go in a mild, thick, smooth snaffle, but in reality—and here I'll probably ruffle some feathers—you'll be kinder to both of you if you use something you aren't constantly hauling on. If your horse is so numb or so heavy that he's completely unresponsive, use a bit that gets some respect and control, such as a thinner snaffle, a Dr. Bristol, or even a slow-twist (remembering that you can't compete in dressage in a slow-twist). If, for example, you're on an old "schoolmaster" who's worked only in a double bridle since he was five, ride in

BUILD YOUR POSITION

1. ESTABLISH. At the halt, line up your shoulder, hip, and heel as my student Courtney King is doing below: stirrup leather on or just behind the vertical (if you're a hunter or jumper rider who pushes so hard into your heel that you brace your foot in front of you, raise the heel and relax your leg until the stirrup is back on the vertical), a little depth in your heel, and a soft angle behind your knee as if you were standing and then squatted just a bit. (Thinking that dressage equals long stirrups is the biggest mistake in the world, by the way. Without angles in your ankle and knee, you lose the shock absorption and security that make your leg quiet and effective.)

2. CONFIRM. To make sure you're in balance and your stirrups aren't too long, rise from the position at left into two-point. (Most of us instinctively want to draw our legs up; two-point makes us let them down.) First, rest your hands on your

BUILD YOUR POSITION
(continued)

horse's neck so you won't hang on his mouth for support. Then, not gripping with your knee or thigh or tightening your back, roll your seat forward out of the saddle. If your stirrup length is right, you'll be balanced so securely that you could stay there forever. If you wobble or something starts to hurt (other than the back of your calf and maybe your ankle—which you're stretching down), sit, relax, realign, and then try two-point again.

3. PRACTICE TWO-POINT at the walk, trot, canter—and in trot-walk transitions, where many people jam their feet forward. At the canter here (right), Courtney is a little too far out of the saddle, so her foot's slipped back a tad, but she's staying in balance (no leaning on her hands) and letting Umego go on his own; he's quiet and calm. If your horse starts to rush, slow him with lots of calming "whoooas" and momentary takes-and-gives on the reins. Slow and give. Slow and give. If that doesn't work, keep using voice and ask him to walk, then trot or canter again. The next time he rushes, use voice and ask him to walk, but only go halfway; then trot or canter in the slower tempo he's given you. (This "halfway to walk" will eventually become your half-halt.)

the double bridle. It'll be easier on everybody. When your dressage vocabulary is bigger and he's conversing with you more, try a snaffle again. And when you do that, don't assume the thickest, mildest bit is best; some horses' mouths aren't that roomy. Ask your equine dentist for advice.

Get Him to "Go on His Own"

You'll never get your horse light to the aids if you use them constantly. Any horse, of any level, should be able to go for periods of time on a loose rein, the way a totally green horse starts his career. So I'm going to take you back to the most basic level of riding and the kind of things you teach a horse the first few times you get on his back: When you put your leg on, he immediately goes forward. He keeps going, without any nagging or thumping, until he hears otherwise from you. And when you say "whoa" and take up on his mouth, he immediately stops.

I'm not talking half-halts, connection, engagement, self-carriage, or

"throughness." I'm talking about the simplest obedience lessons: lessons some horses never learn and even more horses forget along the way.

Sit on your horse with your elbows bent, your hands roughly mirroring the slope of his shoulder, your reins loose, and one hand lightly but firmly closed around the whip with about an inch of handle sticking out (see photo 1 on page 14)—any more and you risk poking yourself in the eye if he bucks and you fall forward. Let the whip lie across your thigh, pointing toward his flank behind your leg, not on his neck or your hip bone. To use the whip, flick your wrist inward with a little snap to it, so the tip touches him without your moving your hand out of position or pulling back on his mouth.

Here's the sequence: At the walk, ask your horse to trot. Think of the aid as a word. Lightly squeeze with your leg for as long as the word takes to say and no longer: "Trot." If he doesn't trot, give him a kick. If he doesn't trot, tap him *once* with the whip (tap-tap-tapping will make him as dull to the whip as he is to your

BELOW: Courtney got left behind a little in the canter depart here—but she's left Umego alone, and that's the point of the challenge. Deliberately riding on a loose rein teaches you not to interfere with your horse and teaches him he can trust you—lessons that Umego's tense body and Courtney's loss of position tell us they both need to learn.

LENDON'S CHALLENGE

Walk, trot, and canter on a loose rein without speeding up and running off. Maintain the walk, trot, and canter without nagging and banging with your leg.

leg). If the tap doesn't work, take the reins in one hand and whap him just once with the whip. He'll probably jump forward, so be ready to throw your hands forward and go with him—you don't want to confuse him by stepping on the accelerator, then stomping on the brake.

Now, because the point is to get him to go from your light leg aid, and not from the punishment of the whip, immediately ask him to return to the walk by giving a little pull that lasts as long as a calm "whoa." If he ignores you or he's so lazy he can't be bothered to stop his momentum, give a little snatch or jerk. Nobody wants to do that, but you've got to get his attention: "Hey, I *spoke* to you, sweetheart!" He may throw his head in the air—but remember, we're not talking about a polished perform-

ance. We're talking about simple obedience: pure "go" and pure "whoa," not finesse.

After three or four tries, your horse should trot off smartly from your light leg aid. When he does, see what he gives you. Leave him alone and don't drop the reins, hang on him, fiddle, seesaw—all of that is interference. You want him to learn to respond to any little move you make, so you have to learn *not* to make moves unless you mean them. Make sure your leg does nothing as well—no kicking or squeezing or thumping! If you absolutely can't resist nagging him, turn your toes in and your heels out (it will feel pretty awkward) so you completely take your leg off. If he breaks to the walk (and he will if he's used to your total support), kick or tap him forward again and say, "No, dear; I said 'TROT'!" ■

A Tool and a Test

1. Use your whip right behind your leg—that's what it's reinforcing!—and be careful not to pull the bit when you do. Here Courtney keeps a soft contact and simply flicks the whip by moving her hand rightward a few inches and rotating her thumb out, keeping her elbow-to-bit line unbroken.

2. This is *not* how you should ride—but it's a great test. At the trot or canter, get into two-point; then, on a loose rein or very soft contact, rotate your knees and toes in so your lower legs come completely off your horse, like this. If he slows or breaks to the walk, you'll know you've been keeping him going by nagging him.

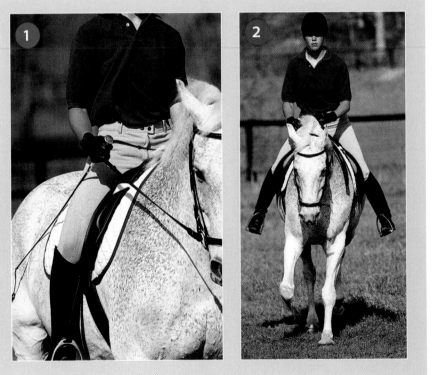

LESSON 2

Passive
Contact

IN LESSON 1, I EXPLAINED THAT you can't hope to ask anything of your horse—be it getting his head down or doing a flying change—until you have the self-awareness and body control to ask (and do) nothing. That means . . .

• going with him without interfering in any way

• speaking to him with your aids only when you mean to

• getting him to go on his own.

But dressage is about communication, and communication can't happen without a connection. So in this lesson we'll move one step closer to communication by developing "passive contact": You're there; you don't do anything to influence your horse; but wherever and however he goes, you follow the natural motion of his head and neck with your hands and the motion of his back with your seat.

Passive contact is what I call "picking

BELOW: To help Courtney figure out how to follow motion very softly, I'm moving my hands on the reins independently of each other, neither rhythmically nor consistently, while she tries to keep a very light contact.

BELOW: Here Courtney's beginning the most difficult step of the canter stride for following: Wonderland is on his inside front leg; his head is at its lowest and her upper body at its farthest back, so she's at greatest risk of catching him in the mouth. But even though she's back a bit far, clearly she's reaching her arms and softly following; there's no pull on his mouth. Inset: If your hands tend to be busy, make them move as one by touching thumbs. Both sides of your horse's jaw move together, so both hands should follow together unless you're making a quick, specific request.

up the telephone." The line is open, you haven't said anything yet, but the potential for communication now exists.

I'll show you how to . . .

• hold your reins to produce an even, consistent, specific contact that your horse can understand (rather than one hand up and one down, or one pulling and one slack)

• follow rein pressure wherever it goes, and not use your hands for security

• carry your upper body erect (and so allow your seat and legs to relax down around him)

• fix the most common problem of all—looking down

• recognize, create, and let go of tension so you *can* relax and follow with your seat.

Hold Your Reins

Place your reins between your thumb and index finger, forming a straight line from the bit through your hand and elbow to your hip and a soft contact that's just short of loose. Keep your fingers closed but not clamped (if your fist is tight, your arm is tight, and you can't follow the motion). I tell my students it's like holding baby birds. If you open your fingers, the birds will fly away; if you tighten your fingers, the birds will get squished. If you widen your hands or hold them unevenly, the birds will get lonely. And if you drop your thumbs, you'll bonk their little heads together.

Now completely turn off your fingers, wrist, and forearm. Do nothing with them. "Take here," "take there," and "wiggle, wig-

LENDON'S CHALLENGE

At the walk, trot, and canter, maintain a passive, light non-interfering contact *wherever your horse puts his head,* be it in the air, to one side, on the ground, or straight out like a dart searching for a dart board. While you do, keep your thumbs touching to prove your hands can move as one—and not take-give-take-give or pull left-right-left-right.

gle, wiggle" isn't learning to be part of your horse. (Besides, our goal at every level is self-carriage, and he can't *give* you self-carriage until you stop asking.)

Follow Rein Pressure

For this next chunk of learning, have a friend play the role of your horse, standing in front of his head and taking hold of the reins behind the bit (as I'm doing in the photo on page 15) so whatever you do won't touch his mouth. Try to keep a light, passive, following contact as she moves the reins back and forth, up and down, left rein, right rein. Have her pull, push, drop the contact, and jerk as if your horse was lurching into a canter transition. (If you can't follow lurches, you can't effectively use your aids to fix them. In fact, this exercise may reveal that you're *making* your horse lurch in order to pull you into the canter.) When you take back to maintain contact, use your upper-arm muscles to pull your hands back softly toward your hip bone (not down toward your thigh). When you give, open your elbow to move your hands toward the bit. And stay relaxed. The more relaxed you are, the better you can go with the range of motion, so your friend never feels she's dragging you, and so you feel you could follow her hands anywhere with a thread between you instead of a piece of leather. (For more practice, stand

LENDON'S CHALLENGE

Position three markers around your ring (I use a ladder, a post, and a door) as "check-your-position" spots. Train yourself, every time you pass those spots, to check yourself for whatever you're working on that day—in this case, it's "eyes up." It can just as easily be "don't hang on the left rein" or "keep your heels down."

LEFT: Courtney's doing the "eyes up" exercise nicely. You can see the positive effect that looking up has on her whole position— and on her happy-looking horse. Another time, the three markers could remind her to work on her hands, checking that her fingers are softly closed as if holding baby birds, not wanting them to fly away but also not wanting to scrunch their little bones.

facing each other on the ground, and use rope or string instead of reins.)

Now transfer that feeling of passive contact to following your horse's head at the walk, trot, and canter. At the trot there won't be much head motion, but your body will have to go up and down while your hands don't. Cantering, at the moment when your horse's forehand is down and your upper body is back, open your elbows and shoulders like hinges; otherwise you'll grab him in the mouth. If you do grab him, put your arms straight forward for a stride and droop your reins. (Be prepared: If he's used to your rigidly holding him, his head may drop to the ground— or he may take off.)

RIGHT: The point in this challenge is not riding a correct transition, but being *able to ride one* because your leg is independent. In downward transitions, so many of us brace on the stirrups or on our knees and thighs, sending our legs in front of us where they can't help us balance. Courtney is basically meeting the challenge well; she's sitting in balance, her upper body very slightly back for the transition into walk, and her horse looks comfortable—though I'd want to see her heel out instead of on his side. (For these heels-out exercises, I tell my students to imagine they're wearing 6-inch spurs that they've got to keep off the horse.) Her arm position is good, too, with that nice straight line from elbow to bit; Wonderland's soft mouth shows she's not depending on him for support.

LENDON'S CHALLENGE

To keep yourself from pushing your seat out of the saddle during trot/walk transitions, turn your heels out and bring your lower legs back and up at almost a 45-degree angle. You may bounce a bit, but that's better than shoving your heels forward and bracing.

Perfect Your Position

Passive contact means "giving" your hand to your horse's mouth, your leg to his side, and your seat to his back. But you retain control of the part of you that creates your position: your upper body. If your chest and head are not up and erect, your upper arms won't have an anchor to hang from, your seat won't be able to relax down onto his back, and your legs won't have a framework from which to hang softly on his sides.

Good upper-body carriage is good posture. You can't expect to sit erect on your horse and slouch around on the ground. Wherever you go, whatever you do, carry your chest up, your rib cage lifted, your chin up, and your head in the middle of your shoulders. Think of me walking up and dropping an ice cube down your back; you'll pull your shoulder blades together, lift your rib cage, and thrust your bust. Or do what I did as a kid: Get a nice big book, put it on top of your head, and walk around. Believe me, if you're tense, crooked, or collapsed, the book won't balance.

Eyes Up!

Looking down destroys . . .

- **accuracy.** Your horse goes where you look. Where is he supposed to go when you look at his neck?
- **posture.** When you look down, your head pulls your shoulders forward, rounds your back, and makes everything collapse.
- **safety.** You're going to run into somebody. (If you've ever competed, you know what it's like to be in the warm-up arena with someone riding as if she's searching for the secret of dressage between her horse's ears.)
- **feel.** I can't tell you how many students tell me, "It's amazing. When I finally raised my eyes, I had so much more

awareness of my horse's body."

You're saying, "OK, Lendon, I'm convinced! Give me an exercise to help me keep my eyes up." Well, it's Lendon's soapbox time again. My answer is an unequivocal "NO!" I refuse to waste my time or yours cooking up exercises or gimmicks. Eyes up just takes DOING. It's not like sitting the trot; *that* takes time and practice. It's not like following your horse's motion; *that* takes feel and "finding it." Eyes up takes pure, unadulterated discipline.

I get as bad as anybody about dropping my eyes, working on my own month after month. But when I catch myself, I overcorrect. I stare at the rafters! I tip my head way, way back and stretch out my neck. I watch the mirrors. I look at other people riding. And when I'm in my outdoor arena—it's in a little bit of a hollow—I focus on the horizon. If I can keep my eyes up, you can, too. If you can't, you need a little bonk over the head.

Let Go of Tension

Stiffening your back keeps you from sitting the trot and going with your horse at the canter. Clamping your thighs and tightening your buttock muscles squeezes you out of the saddle. Here's a simple way to release tension (as Courtney demonstrates on page 20): At the walk, squeeze your buttocks and thigh muscles as tight as you can, until you're almost pushing your seat up and away from your horse. Now relax as if sitting on your couch in front of the TV; let your muscles soften, spread, and cover as much of your saddle as possible. Let your seat bones open, sink down through your muscles, and melt into the leather. Don't force it. Let it happen. You don't *make* yourself sit on the couch. You just sink into the cushions. Squeeze again—tight, tighter—hold for a moment, and then relax and sink into the couch. That's "letting go." You can do it with any part of your body, at any time. Right now, feel it in your seat, your thighs, your back, and keep the feeling as you move into the trot and canter.

Let Go for Downward Transitions

Go from trot to walk by maintaining a passive, light contact with the reins; stopping posting; "letting go" in your seat, thighs, and back; and thinking "walk." If your horse doesn't respond, say, "Walk." If he trots on, check him: Pull back with your upper arms so the reins move an inch or two toward your hip; then immediately release. Remember, aids are words, and your pull should last no longer than the word "walk." If he still doesn't walk, pull or jerk harder and more quickly, but immediately release. You don't want to teach him that he doesn't have to shift his weight back to stop but can just lean on your hand.

After letting go, the biggest thing to remember about canter-to-trot—a fairly major transition—is not to interfere with your horse. He may fall on his forehand and run a little; let it happen. Don't catch him in the mouth in the name of "well, he's hurrying." Relax, don't interfere, and make your adjustment when you're in control of your body.

Go and Play

Sometimes, the more you think, the less you feel—so I'm going to shut up now and let you explore passive contact on your own. As you do, make sure your reins never droop and you never look like Godzilla, with your muscles bulging. Make sure that, if I were watching, the bit would appear absolutely immobile in your horse's mouth. Feel a light connection at all times, as if no matter what he does (within reason), you are part of it.

Don't worry about how your horse is going. At this point, he's merely a vehicle. In Lesson 1, you got him to go on his own. In this lesson, go with him—even if he cuts corners, pops his shoulder, or holds his head in some really strange place. Just keep your hand, leg, and seat as soft and connected as possible. Until you can truly be part of him, the rest is irrelevant. ∎

Let Go of Tension

SQUEEZE. First, Courtney squeezes her buttock muscles with everything she's got. You can see her seat come up off the saddle—but look beyond that, at the accompanying tension in her neck and back and shoulders! We didn't tell her to tighten there; we just told her to tighten her seat. But if you tighten one part of your body, chances are you'll have tension elsewhere.

RELAX. Now she completely relaxes her buttock muscles—and look at the change in her whole body. Yes, her head has dropped a little too much, but that's the exercise: total relaxation. See the difference!

LESSON 3

Active
Contact . . . With Legs

LENDON'S CHALLENGE

On a circle, move your horse away from your inside leg by leg alone—without changing your upper body, your hands, or the weight on his back. You're not using your seat in any way, just your leg.

Here's an example of the active contact we'll be developing in this lesson. Courtney's right leg is just slightly back from the girth. That's the right place for pushing Scenic's whole body left; farther back, the aid would talk just to his hind leg. In response, he's not just stepping across with his inside hind; he's moving his whole body away. She's following his mouth, putting no pressure on the bit, and her right hand is open enough that we can see she's not trying to push him over with the reins. If you were lokking from behind (as the page 22 photo shows), you'd see that Courtney is sitting pretty straight in the middle of his back. She's keeping her left (outside) leg passive, just "there"—not shoving it in front of her, a common mistake. Scenic's quiet tail shows he's accepting the exercise.

Scenic crosses over in front in response to Courtney's right-leg pressure.

BY DEVELOPING THE ABILITY TO DO (and ask) nothing and to maintain passive contact, the basic skills we covered in the first two lessons, you've done what I call "picking up the telephone." You've opened the line. You haven't said anything yet, but you've started to tune in to your horse and create the potential for clear, cordial, ungarbled communication, free of confusing static and interference.

Now We Start Communicating

In this lesson, I'll show you how to create "active contact" between your leg aids and your horse's hindquarters, one leg at a time. The simplest way to do this is to teach him to move away from your leg—not with a classic, formal leg-yield, but with something similar to what you do when you're in his stall mucking out and you put your hand or finger on his side and push to tell him to move out of the way.

The exercise I'll give you just takes that moving-over reaction one step further, getting a no-big-deal response when you use pressure from one leg to tell your horse, "Go that way." This basic leg-yielding skill will help you get a positive reaction from him, develop energy, and (later on) create a round frame.

I'm going to give you four different ways to encourage your horse's hindquarters to respond to your leg aids . . .

- at the walk on a circle
- at the walk on the wall or fence
- with a turn on the forehand under saddle
- with a turn on the forehand from the ground.

Now, I'm not giving you four ways to get a response because I want you to do each and every one. I'm giving you four ways because . . .

If One Ain't Workin' . . .

. . . you stop doin' it and try another. This is probably the most important piece of training advice I can share with you. I don't know you, and I don't know your horse, so I cannot give you an exact formula for what's always going to work for the two of you. All I can do is give you alternatives to play with—and even then I can't say for sure that any of them will work. But the bottom line is this: *You never want your horse to ignore or turn down a question or request.*

Horses are creatures of habit. They learn by repetition. If you ask your horse to "whoa" ten or twelve times and he doesn't do it, you haven't just failed at getting him to stop; you've taught him to ignore you and keep going! So anytime you find yourself asking, begging, and pleading for a positive response—and by that I mean you're not getting the reaction you want within two requests—stop, get help, back off and do something you can both succeed at, or figure out another way to ask. (You already know that what you're doing isn't working; in my book, analyzing the why and wherefore isn't particularly important.) In short, do anything you can think of to make sure your training program confirms only good habits in your horse.

Leg-Yield on the Circle

Track right on a walk circle that's a bit smaller than the width of your ring. Maintain passive rein contact by following the natural motion of your horse's head and neck, and ask him to yield to your leg: Put

your right leg back a couple of inches, without lifting your heel, and give him a little squeeze or tap that says, "Please move sideways and make the circle a tiny bit bigger."

If you've laid a proper groundwork with your first two lessons, your horse will probably react by speeding up. That's actually good, and understandable, because up until now you've told him that leg pressure means "go faster," and he really doesn't

Make the job of meeting the "Lendon's Challenge" below easier—as Courtney's done—by approaching the fence at a 45-degree angle and keeping the haunches in, instead of trying to push them in. Her pulsating right leg asked Scenic to cross over behind just as his right hind leg was coming up—the ideal moment—and he responded; now he's about to cross over in front. (Have a helper tell you each time the hind leg leaves the ground until you feel it instinctively—which you will with practice.) Courtney's right hand is a little too close to the neck to have the direct elbow-to-mouth line and the nice contact we look for, but she isn't pulling on him.

LENDON'S CHALLENGE

Ask for a leg-yield along the fence or wall while trying to feel the right hind and asking that leg, specifically, to cross over. If your horse tenses and his head goes up, just follow it.

BELOW: 1. Starting parallel to the rail, Courtney's moved her right leg back a little to ask Scenic to move left, and he's already started crossing right hind in front of left. This is the moment when a horse is most liable to move straight ahead. In checking Scenic, Courtney's dropped her right hand a little instead of keeping her pressure even and steadying him back.

2. Doing the turn one step at a time, they're almost perpendicular to the fence. Courtney has steadied Scenic and returned to a soft contact. He's above the bit, but that's irrelevant here.

3. Here the loop in the rein shows it's clearly not holding him. Her right leg is just slightly back, pressing him to finish the turn. Look back through this sequence and you'll see that Scenic's front legs are pretty much moving up and down in place (look at his left front in photo 2, for example)—which is just right.

have the vocabulary to differentiate between two legs working at the same time and one leg working by itself. If he does speed up, quietly say, "Whoa," pull back on both reins, and then immediately release without holding him. HOLDING HIM IS SOMETHING YOU MUST NEVER DO. Give another squeeze or tap with your right leg; if he doesn't move his haunches a tiny bit sideways, add a touch with the whip on his flank, right behind your boot. If he moves over a tiny bit, ask again with a squeeze in time with his walk—what I call a "pulsating leg." As soon as he gives you a positive response of two or three steps, pat him, praise him, let him walk straight ahead, change rein, and try leg-yielding on a circle to the left.

Most horses will give some sort of fumbling but positive leg-yield response on a circle. If yours isn't one of them—he ignores your leg entirely, or runs forward, or even kicks at your leg—cut your losses immediately by moving on to . . .

Leg-Yield on the Wall (or Fence)

Track left at the walk and approach the wall or fence at a 45-degree angle. As you arrive, briefly feel your horse's mouth (to tell him you're not simply going to turn onto the track) and, with your right leg back a couple of inches, give a light squeeze or tap on his side to tell him you want him to hold the angle and move away from your leg. Let the wall do most

LENDON'S CHALLENGE

Concentrate again on sitting straight as you ask your horse to move his quarters around his forehand—and think about doing each step individually, so that you could stop after each if you wanted.

of the job of controlling his tendency to rush off. As much as possible, make sure your hands just follow passively; if he does try to hurry down the track, feel his mouth with even pressure on both reins, just enough to steady him, and then soften again. You're not supposed to turn or pull his head to the side; this exercise is about *leg*-yield, not rein-yield. If he gives no response to your leg, ask again and add a touch of the whip. If this doesn't work, walk a circle, come back to face the wall head-on, and try a . . .

Turn on the Forehand Under Saddle

Start by riding a 90-degree turn. Facing the wall, head-on, put your right leg back and

squeeze or tap to ask your horse to move his haunches one step to the left. Keep your hands passive; the wall will prevent him from rushing forward. Again, pulling his head around is not the point—getting a response to your hands teaches him nothing about responding to your leg. (Later, when he's reliable in this exercise, you'll ask for a 180-degree turn from a start parallel to the rail—see "Lendon's Challenge" at left and the photos below. Your hands still will do nothing but follow his natural motion and briefly correct him if he tries to walk forward.)

If your horse doesn't move to the left, reinforce your leg aid with a tap of the whip. If that doesn't work, ask Great-Aunt Gertie to come out, stand next to your

Courtney's pressing just where her calf would lie, and Scenic's stepping around with no resistance. She's using no rein pressure—pulling his head toward her would make his haunches move but teach him nothing about the leg.

right leg, and poke her thumb in your horse's ribs to encourage him to move over. If even Great-Aunt Gertie doesn't get results (I've had some horses who were super-tough about learning this lesson), get off and try a . . .

Turn on the Forehand on the Ground

Stand on your horse's right side, with the

reins in your right hand, and give him a nudge with your left thumb just behind the girth, where your calf normally rests. Again, the response doesn't have to be anything formal. All I care about is that when you put your thumb (and later your leg) on him, he listens to it and moves away. Keep it rhythmical and steady: nudge-step-nudge-step-nudge-step.

Just two or three steps is all I'm asking.

LENDON'S CHALLENGE

If your horse didn't move away from your leg in the first three challenges, dismount and get him to move away from thumb pressure just behind the girth.

That's no big deal. When your horse gives it to you easily and seems to understand, get back on and try it with your leg reinforced by your whip. You will have accomplished what this exercise wants when he tells you, by his positive response, that he understands: Leg pressure on one side means "move away."

How Long Should You Work?

I'm glad you asked that question! The moment you have some success—your horse tells you he has the idea of leg-yield by giving you a few willing, comfortable steps—praise him with voice and pats, and leave it.

You aren't asking for anything dramatic, but you *are* asking for something new and different. That can be surprisingly discouraging for a horse, even when he gets it right. He feels a mental strain in trying to figure it out, and a physical strain in trying to get his muscles to stretch and work a new way—and you don't want him to hate what he's doing. You never want him to see you coming and go to the back of his stall, muttering to himself, "Uh-oh. Here she is again with another hour of drill, drill, drill."

Remember, you're doing dressage because it's something YOU want to do. Making your horse perform better means a lot to you but means nothing to him. He's only doing it out of respect for you and the pure kindness of his heart, so it's up to you to make certain he's happy about his work and proud of what he's learning. You want him to say, "Hey! What I just did was pretty nifty!! I'm really smart!"

How to keep your horse happy? When you're riding, use lots of voice and touch to praise him. However, the biggest reward you can ever give him is to *stop*

working him. Take him out of the ring, take him on the trail, take him back to the barn, and let him know he's done something wonderful.

Knowing when to quit is more than just a matter of keeping your horse happy, by the way. It's how you avoid disaster. I've seen this mistake so many times: Your horse figures out how to move off your leg. What you should do is praise him and say, "Hey, this is great. He's got it. Now all I have to do is not let him do it incorrectly even once. I'm going to quit while we're ahead." But instead, you say, "Gee—we can really do this. We're hot stuff!" And you pound away at it until you blow it.

This kind of mistake is a particular danger if you're an amateur who's trying to be disciplined about fitting riding into your busy schedule. You can easily make the mistake of thinking that when you've set aside an hour to school, you have to school for an hour. But you don't. Many's the time I'll get off a horse after three or four minutes of riding—because he's come out and done perfectly something that had been a stumbling block before. When that kind of breakthrough happens, I get away from it as fast as I can. I quit while I'm ahead because I don't want to keep going until I run into trouble.

But what if the inevitable happens and you find yourself in trouble before you can help it? Whatever you do, don't drill and drill and drill. Back off. Do something you *know* you and your horse can do well. Get his confidence back. Then coax him along by saying, "Come on. You can do this, you will do this"—but always say it in an upbeat, positive fashion. ■

> " The biggest reward you can ever give your horse is to *stop working him*."

LENDON'S CHALLENGE

Your horse can create a "false" sense of bend by ducking his chin toward his chest or shoulder. Check that his poll stays the same height, and that the outside of his neck stretches and gets longer. If his poll drops and his neck shortens, he's not bending correctly.

LESSON 4

Active Contact...With Hands

IN THIS LESSON, WE'LL CREATE active contact between your hand aids (with a little help from your leg) and your horse's mouth. The best way to do this is to teach him that when you take on one rein, he bends his neck and turns his head toward that rein. No big deal. You're not after a bend through his body. You're not asking for engagement of his inside hind leg. You're just asking for a basic response that will help you to . .

• get a positive reaction and encourage him to work with you

• teach him to stretch the outside of his body

• reveal such rider problems as pulling and/or such horse evasions as bracing or rolling up

• (with the help of these qualities) get him to round his neck, give his jaw, and place his head near the vertical.

Once he's responding to your leg and hand, you'll have all sorts of ways to encourage him to come on the bit with his face on the vertical and an arch to his neck.

First, let's differentiate between . . .

Good Hands and Educated Hands

We've already worked on passive contact—or what the nineteenth-century horseman James Fillis called "good hands": hands that give when the horse takes and take when the horse gives. Now we're getting to active contact, or what Fillis called "educated hands": They take when the horse takes and give when he gives. For example, you take on the left rein, your horse gives by bending left, and you immediately reward him by giving back. If he doesn't bend left, you maintain the pressure; you give back only when he gives.

I'll show you two ways to encourage your horse to soften his jaw in response to your rein aids (and start developing "educated hands" as you do): by teaching him to bend his neck to the inside and outside on a circle and (if that doesn't work) by doing a "dramatic" leg-yield on a circle. (This is a nice way of describing what a dressage judge would call a "very bad" leg-yield: You'll permit your horse's shoulder to bulge and his neck to overbend in order to show him that he can soften his jaw.)

This exercise is a perfect example of why . . .

Dressage Purists May Sniff . . .

. . . at some things I tell you. Well, I'll be the first to admit that I don't always use the most classical techniques. But purely classical techniques don't always help amateurs who may have horses with difficult conformation or holes in their training, and who—as you may—work at home, on their own, where they don't have or maybe can't afford regular professional help from a qualified trainer.

BENDING TO THE INSIDE ON A CIRCLE
In the photo at left, Courtney's legs are staying close to Cody. She's using a leading rein, moving her hand to the inside and back just enough to turn his head to the inside. He's bending from the shoulder forward, with his whole neck, giving us the sense that she has a nice contact on both reins— that her active inside arm is not rigid and her outside arm is softly allowing the bend without throwing the rein away. Except for being turned a little to the inside, his head and neck are in the same basic position that they would have been for going straight. His poll hasn't dropped, and his nose isn't ducked in. But not all bends are so successful, as you'll see on the next page.

With Hands

A FALSE SENSE OF BEND
This is a wonderfully bad picture of a common problem. Cody has brought his head to the inside in response to the rein; but instead of stretching the outside of his neck and making it longer, he's dropped his poll—it's no longer the highest point of his body—and is giving DOWN rather than around and out in front of him to the right. (At least he's coming to the inside. Many horses *just* drop their polls!) Part of the problem may be the indirect rein Courtney's using: She's bringing her right rein against the neck, instead of bringing it away from the neck in a leading rein like the one that produced the correct bend in our previous photo. In the long run, this false-bend problem only gets worse if not corrected: You'll see horses doing half-passes with very short, jammed-up, flexed necks. A horse that gives only the jaw is hard to fix, too; getting him to come to the bit is more difficult than getting a horse who's a little tough to soften.

For example, experience tells me that when you tug on the reins to ask your horse to stop, he probably braces and gives back some pressure. I could bark, "Get him on the bit; drive him forward with your leg; close your fingers; and *make* him step deeper underneath, soften his topline, and flex at the poll"—but, my friend, it ain't gonna happen. I can talk half-halts and engagement and "classical" riding from back to front until I'm blue in the face, but that critter won't lighten up until you find a system for separating his big, strong, uneducated body into smaller parts—hind end, middle, front end—that you can talk to and control individually (and, therefore, more easily).

I've been giving you just such a system. The "go" and "whoa" response helped you control your horse's hind end. Leg-yielding improved that control and helped you to place the middle of his body. Bending will help you actively communicate with his front end: nothing fancy or formal; just one more low-key/no-big-deal way to get him working with you instead of against you.

Besides, when you finally put the pieces together, you *will* ride your horse from back to front. You may not have achieved it the purely classical way, but you'll have something no purist can sniff at: a correct, responsive, willing partner.

Bending to the Inside on a Circle

Pick up a marching, rhythmic walk on a 20-meter circle to the right. Maintain passive contact on both reins. Lightly position your outside left leg a touch behind the girth, and "pulse" your right leg on the girth to keep your horse energetically walking forward and on the track. (He'll probably want to follow his nose and turn in on the circle when he starts to bend.)

Now ask him to soften his jaw and bend his nose to the inside: Bring your right hand slightly to the inside and your elbow back, and "allow" your left arm to move forward so he turns his nose far enough right that you see his right eye and he stretches the left side of his neck.

Be forewarned: He probably won't give. If he doesn't, don't cave in—you'll just teach him to brace and pull. Instead, maintain your contact and MAKE IT HAPPEN. Be clearer, stronger, and more insistent. Raise your inside hand enough to place the bit in the corner of his lips, where he *can't* brace. (If you lower your hand, you put the bit on the bars, where he CAN get stronger than you.) Halt if you must, keep your legs firmly on his sides so he doesn't back up, drop the left rein and use both hands on the right rein—anything you need to do to get him to give to the pressure and turn his head to the right. The *instant* he does—and all you're asking at this point is a simple response—immediately soften, not by flinging the rein away but by smoothly returning to passive contact.

Now, let me explain something. In my book, "bend" is an active verb. Your horse's head shouldn't "twwwwang" straight as soon as you soften. Just as he should pick up a trot when you tell him to and trot until you say otherwise, he should bend when you tell him to and stay bent without your prompting for at least a few strides. Otherwise, you'll just be back in the old self-carriage dilemma: How can he maintain a bend if you hold it for him?

Bending to the Outside on a Circle

At the walk, rhythmically pulse your outside (left) leg on the girth to maintain ener-

> "When you finally put the pieces together, you *will* ride your horse from back to front."

THE "DRAMATIC" LEG-YIELD

Here Courtney's brought her inside leg back a little more than in the "basic bend," helping her push Cody's barrel sideways and move his body farther out on the circle than his face. Her hand is out in a good leading rein, and—very important—she's sitting evenly, not collapsing her inside shoulder or hip as she presses him outward. He's giving her the correct "incorrect" response, doing exactly what she's told him to do: pushing his shoulder way out (something we want just for now; we'll learn to control it as we advance), making the left side of his body much longer than the right. His poll is a touch low, but his nose is clearly out; he's at no risk of ducking behind.

LENDON'S CHALLENGE

Can you bend your horse, at any time, with your inside hand well away from—not pressing into—his neck, so that you're controlling his body with your inside leg, not with an inside rein against his neck?

gy and prevent your horse from turning off the track, out of the circle, when you ask him to bend: Open and take back with your outside (left) hand, and move your inside (right) hand forward until he softens his jaw and you can see his left eye. Hold the contact until he gives—and as soon as he does, immediately reward him by returning both hands to passive contact.

Once your horse readily responds to your hand (and your supporting leg) by bending his neck and softening his jaw to the inside and outside in both directions, give him a break. (Whenever you teach something new, remember, leave it the moment he gets the idea.) Then go back and try it on the circle at the trot and the canter. Add this bending to your warm-up as a loosening exercise and a reminder to your horse that he should always respond to your active hand by softening his jaw and bending his neck.

If your horse has spent years being rigid and unyielding, and he's so stuck that you just can't break through his resistance on a circle, move on to . . .

The "Dramatic" Leg-Yield

As I told you earlier, this is an effective exercise—it allows you to get a bend by pushing your horse's body out on a wider circle than his head—but it makes for a lousy leg-yield, because you allow him to fall out through his outside shoulder. Right now, though, it's a practical means to an end for a horse who's uncommonly unyielding. So use it with my blessing—but as soon as you get the simple yielding response you're looking for, leave the "dramatic" leg-yield forever behind you. (In Lesson 6 I'll give you an exercise that, among other things, helps you start gaining control over bulging, leaning, falling-in, or falling-out shoulders.)

Track right on a medium-size circle in an energetic, marching walk. Maintain passive rein contact, sit up and evenly on both seat bones (so you don't collapse your inside shoulder or hip), and place your outside (left) leg a bit behind the girth to keep your horse's haunches from leading. Now ask him to make the circle a bit bigger by leg-yielding out: Bring your inside hand a little bit to the inside and slightly back, move your outside hand forward—and every time his inside (right) hind leg leaves the ground to begin its forward/sideways step, press your inside leg on or close behind the girth. (If you're not sure you can feel when that foot comes up, have a friend watch and tell you, "Now . . . now . . . now . . . ") Your horse should step his left foreleg diagonally forward and sideways, lead with his left shoulder, stretch his outside, overbend his neck, and move his body farther out than his head, giving his jaw. As soon as he does, return to passive contact and walk energetically forward on the circle.

Try it again and again until he starts to understand softening and giving. Then return to simple bending, to the inside and the outside, on the circle.

As you work on these two exercises, remember that ultimately, when you bend your horse correctly, you'll use a little bit of each one: a little bit of directing his head with your hand (the opening inside rein), a little bit of directing his body with your inside leg. Those are the subtleties you're working toward. By accomplishing these exercises, you'll be well on your way. ■

LENDON'S CHALLENGE

When your horse responds to your half-go, does your connection stay the same? If it does, you're neither throwing him away nor blocking him from going forward; you're energizing him with your leg.

"Half-Goes" and "Half-Halt Ideas"

NOW WE'RE GOING TO INCREASE your coordination and sharpen your horse's responses. According to classical dressage precepts, we should do this with a half-halt—you increase your leg aid to create more energy that you immediately contain and redirect with your hand.

But—you know me! —I think classical half-halts scare people to death. So I ease into them with two simple precursors:
1. "Half-goes"—they emphasize the energizing leg action.
2. "Half-halt ideas"—they emphasize the containing, redirecting hand action.

And I teach each one in two doable steps: first on a straight line, where you can focus on the forward and back response; then on a circle, where you can build those aids by maintaining a bend.

"But, Lendon," you're asking, "isn't this just a rehash of 'go and whoa' and passive and active contact?"

Not really. Here's what's new and different about half-goes and half-halt ideas:

• You accomplish them within two strides, so both you and your horse are sharper and more on the ball.

• You start coordinating leg and hand aids that you've used only individually before—and influencing body parts you've controlled only separately.

On the straight line, for example, there'll be no more telling your horse to go forward by dropping his mouth and kicking, and no more telling him to come back by taking your leg off and pulling. On the cir-

cle, there'll be no more ignoring his head if it flies in the air; you'll maintain passive contact on the outside rein and create a slightly active bending contact with your inside rein and leg. When you take an active feel on the reins to ask him to come back, you'll maintain an equally active leg contact.

Soon you'll have all the ingredients that help you develop half-halts: willingness to go forward and come back, and the suppleness that comes from bending. And you will have acquired them the way I like: simply, clearly, and without confusion or frustration.

Before we get to the how-to, let's take a look at . . .

What a Half-Halt Actually Is

• It's a call to attention, a small adjustment, a "yoo-hoo!" to your horse.

• It's a powerful tool that improves whatever your horse is doing now, or alerts him to figures, movements, or transitions that are coming up.

• It's an energizing action that gets your horse to use his hind end and step under his body with more quickness and power.

But it's never, never, NEVER what we all too often see—an isolated, unsupported, out-of-the-blue yank on your horse's mouth, or hanging or squeezing for dear life. (The only way it can be a *half*-halt is if your aids subside as soon as you get a response.)

HALF-GOES
The photo at left shows a marvelous moment. Courtney's looking straight ahead and sitting right in the middle of her horse, not collapsing in any direction. She has a lovely softness to her arms (I'm not sure why her right hand is higher than her left) and a straight line from elbow to bit. Look at the bit and you'll clearly see that, even though she's got contact, she's not pulling on Cody's mouth. She's closed her leg exactly where she should to ask him to go forward, and everything from the activity of his legs to his expression—ears forward, tail flowing softly behind him—says, "I'm responding willingly and unresistingly, taking bigger, more energetic steps."

POSTING WITHOUT STIRRUPS

Looking quickly, you'd think Michele was using her stirrups. Her leg is correct, and she's rising out of the saddle easily, not sticking her elbows out or leaning forward. Her upper body and arms are very relaxed, even though she's gripping with her lower leg. Her ear, shoulder, hip, and heel are nicely aligned. And she has a pleasant contact and isn't pulling herself up on Aastrakhan's mouth (a common fault). The mare's relaxed look says Michele's probably not slamming into her in the "down" phase of posting, either. Use this moment to identify the muscles you grip with—so later you can "let go" of them to encourage the relaxation that will let you sit down into the saddle at the sitting trot.

to learn by what Centered Riding guru Sally Swift calls "attrition"—trying until you get shaken into it.

In fact, I figure sitting trot is like the half-halt—something you never stop studying and learning. So I've divided our introduction to sitting trot into three progressive and doable lessons.

In this first lesson, we'll start increas-

ing your security and relaxation, and suppling and strengthening you and your horse, by . . .

• teaching you the feel of sitting down on your seat bones and not gripping for security, something we'll do with *leg lifts at the walk*

• building your strength without losing relaxation; teaching you to secure your

LENDON'S CHALLENGE

Do your feet stay in the same place as you post without stirrups? Are you keeping your arms quietly by your sides as you post?

position with your upper calf, knee, and lower thigh; and (a sneaky little stratagem on my part) fatiguing your muscles so you relax and let go—all of which we'll accomplish through *posting trot without stirrups*

• and—because all the exercises in the world won't help you sit if your horse's back muscles are too stiff and weak to support you—strengthening and suppling him by means of *jogging up low hills*.

Next? Ideally, we'll put you on the longe to learn sitting trot (although I'll show you another way if that's just not possible), because there are times when you need to focus completely on yourself and your seat. But we can't do that until your horse is a safe, steady, and schooled longe horse. So in Lesson 8 you'll continue strengthening and suppling while you turn him into a good longeing partner. (For riding on the longe, you'll need a knowledgeable friend or professional holding the longe line. If you have such a person, great; if he or she has a well-schooled longe horse, even better. But if you can't find anyone to help you, teach your horse to longe anyway. Longeing is one of the best ways to produce a stronger, suppler, rounder dressage partner who's easier to sit.)

Finally, in the third part of this "mini-series," on the longe (or on passive contact if you have to work on your own), we'll utilize your newly developed relaxation, strength, and suppleness to ease you into a sitting trot where you move comfortably with your horse and don't go against him. (You *will* fall apart and bounce sometimes—we all do—so I'll also give you some effective fixes.)

You'll want to let your horse be a "vehicle" for these exercises. Ride him on passive contact—or, if he's just wonderful, on a loose rein. The focus here is *you*, and you can't think about your position and his

roundness or bend while you're learning something new. So, as long as he's safe, sit there, work on yourself, let him trundle along and carry you, and forget about how he's going, because the rest really doesn't matter.

Do Leg Lifts at the Walk . . .

. . . to help you find your seat bones and give yourself the feel of sitting down and around your horse.

First, make sure that your heel, hip, and shoulder line up, and that you have some depth in your heel and a soft angle behind your knee. Then check that you're carrying your upper body so your back is basically straight. Your upper body is yours to carry; what it does depends totally on you. When your chest and eyes are up, your hips and legs can naturally hang downward. You want to give them over to your horse, relax them, and make them part of him. Our goal is for *your seat to become part of his back*.

When you're ready, lift your left knee far enough upward to raise your leg, from calf to hip, off the saddle; then *immediately* lower it again. Don't try to hold the lift; you'll rotate onto the back of your butt. You want it to be a very quick thing, literally as fast as the words "up, down": just long enough to put you on your seat bones, "unglue" your leg, and break your grip. (Your leg really has nothing to do with staying on your horse. As I tell my students, "If I amputated your legs 4 inches down from your hips, I'd expect you to sit exactly the same.")

Feel how the lift puts you "on and into" the saddle, with relaxed buns and with the same feel of "give" you experience when you go from trot to walk—and how

"Our goal is for *your seat to become part of his back*."

your leg lies softly on your horse's side without holding or gripping, very much the same way your hand softly contacts his mouth. Lift each leg two or three times, lift both legs together, and get into the habit of doing a quick, imperceptible leg lift whenever you feel your seat getting tight or your leg clamping.

Post Without Stirrups
*. . . to build your strength, improve your secur-*ity, and deepen your seat by tiring your gripping muscles.

Let me explain. Former USET three-day-eventing coach Jack Le Goff used to tell us (yes, I trained with the three-day team in 1969 and '70, in my eventing days!) that when he was head of Saumur, the French Cavalry School, they'd put a raw, young, never-been-on-a-horse-before recruit on the longe, without reins or stirrups, and have him trot and canter until his

JOGGING LOW HILLS
Freed up by Michele's off-the-saddle position, Aastrakhan is showing just what we're looking for: a wonderful stride and tremendous athleticism. The mare is moving with obvious power, her bending joints and the freedom of her shoulder giving a strong sense of how she's "pushing" up that hill; and she's stretching down into the bridle, making full use of her back. You sense, too, that if the reins broke, Michele wouldn't fall backward—because she's not depending on them for balance.

LENDON'S CHALLENGE

Does your horse feel as if he's pulling himself along with his front feet, or as if a powerful engine is pushing him with rhythm from behind?

horse was tired. Then they'd bring out another horse, and another, and another, until the poor kid was so exhausted there wasn't a muscle in his body he could tense—and he'd sit beautifully. The point: You can't *make* yourself sit. You have to *let* yourself sit. Posting without stirrups is another way to learn how.

I don't like to see banging stirrups, so remove yours or cross them over as shown on page 44. Make sure your heel, hip, and shoulder line up, you have enough angle behind your knee to rise out of the saddle, and your foot is where it would be if you had your stirrups. Trot, keeping your lower leg fairly passive against your horse's side; grip with your upper calf, inner knee, and lower thigh (one of the few times I'll tell you to grip!) and allow his bounce to push you out of the saddle. Softly sit again, momentarily relax your upper calf, inner knee, and lower thigh muscles to let everything go; then grip as you rise with his bounce once more. Hey! No flapping arms. The lift has to be from your legs, so keep your elbows by your sides.

If you start to tip sideways, lose your balance, or pull up your knees, hold the pommel for a moment to regroup. (Don't hold all the time, though. That would be a crutch, not a correction.) If you absolutely can't fix your position at the trot, or if you've gone beyond relaxation and you're too exhausted to continue, walk—because Lendon's Rule still obtains: If it ain't workin', go back to what you *can* do, regroup, and find some success. (And this, my friend, is as true for teaching piaffe as it is for aligning your heel, hip, and shoulder.)

When you take breaks in the walk, let your legs just hang down so that you completely relax the muscles on the insides of your thighs, your seat, and the tissues that push your knees into the sad-dle. Let everything go, and allow your seat to come as deep into the saddle as it will in the walk. This is the relaxation you're going to use in sitting trot.

This exercise may not sound like a whole lot of fun, but it pays great dividends: The muscles you grip with to post without stirrups are the very muscles that, when tight, prevent you from sitting the trot. Posting without stirrups will quickly let you recognize them: They're the ones that hurt! Once you recognize those muscles, you can relax them. As they start to hurt, you're going to say, "Oh, I want to let that go." When you do "let that go," you'll be able to sit the trot. If you squeeze yourself away from the saddle, you cannot sit.

Jog up Low Hills . . .

. . . to get out of the arena, have a little fun, broaden your experience, and start strengthening and suppling your horse's back to withstand your sitting trot.

Keep your knee and thigh soft and your back relaxed as you roll your seat forward out of the saddle until you're balanced over your leg in the two-point jumping position we worked on in our first lesson. Trot up a gently sloping hill, looking for the same frame, relaxation, rhythm, and obedience you have in the arena—ideally, with your horse's neck stretched low out of his withers and his face close to the vertical, because that's when you can really influence the muscles underneath you. If he gives you the feeling that a powerful engine is pushing from behind, he's telling you he's tracking up, each hind foot is stepping in the print of the forefoot on the same side—and he isn't dragging himself with his front feet while his hind feet dawdle along (which would do nothing to make him stronger). ■

TACK UP . . .

1. Attaching the longe line so it goes through the inside bit ring, over the head, and snaps to the outside bit ring creates downward pressure over the poll and upward pressure on the bit. That's too much control for some horses (see photo 2 for the milder alternative), but not for a bully, an extremely fresh horse, or a horse I've never longed before. The elastic strap over the saddle is one great way to secure run-up stirrups so they don't bang against a horse's sides.

2. This milder attachment, snapping the longe line to the inside bit ring, may give too little control if Jamboree opens his mouth or pulls so hard to the outside that the bit slides through (though the flash or drop noseband should prevent that). With either attachment, I secure the bridle reins out of the way: First, as you see in photo 1, I put them over his neck as if to ride him. Then I pick them up under his throat, wrap them around and around each other until they're twisted fairly tight, pass the throatlatch through one rein, and buckle it. With the bridle reins high on the bit, where they can't interfere, I can attach the side reins below them.

LESSON 8

Create a Good
Longe Partner

IN LESSON 7, WE BEGAN PREPARING for sitting trot by increasing your security and strengthening and suppling you and your horse. For the next step, ordinarily I'd put you on the longe, where you could focus on yourself and your seat. But I don't want to do that until we know your horse is a reliably safe longe partner, and until we know he's supple and strong in his back. (I must tell you: Some horses never become reliable longe partners. If yours is one of them, you can longe him to build his suppleness and strength, but you'll also need to find a safe "schoolmaster" type that you

can have some longe lessons on.)

So in this lesson we'll take a recess from the "you" stuff to . . .

- discuss proper longeing equipment
- discuss safety (so you never end up with a longe line wrapped around your arm and your horse dragging you down the driveway)
- teach your horse to accept side reins and stretch his neck forward and round his back
- check that he's tracking up—stepping his hind feet in the prints of his front feet
- determine whether he's pushing from

3. Don't have an elastic strap to keep stirrups still? Run up the iron with the leather on the outside; loop the leather under the iron, up, over itself, around the front branch of the iron, behind itself, and toward the rear branch; then pass the free end through and tuck it into its keeper to lock the iron in place.

4. Loop—NEVER COIL—the longe line back and forth across the palm of your hand. I've heard of way too many injuries (and at least one death) from a line wrapping tight around someone's hand when a horse bolted or shied. And DON'T hold all the line in one hand. Put the extra in the hand toward your horse's tail and feed it out through the hand toward his head. This method takes time and a little practice to get comfortable and quick with, especially when you're holding a whip, but it's well worth the effort because it is the safest.

behind (which is what you want) or pulling along from in front (which is what you don't want).

Then in Lesson 9, we'll put you up on this wonderful longe horse (yours or your borrowed schoolmaster).

Again, you will need a knowledgeable friend or professional to longe you. Even if you don't have such a person, doing the longe lesson we're about to start will improve your horsemanship and give you a stronger, suppler, rounder dressage partner who's easier to sit. And you can just do Lesson 9's exercises as you did Lesson 7's: on passive contact—or, if your horse trundles along, on a completely loose rein. (You can't, in all fairness, think about your position *and* his bend.)

Longeing Pointers

• If your horse is stiff or has bad hocks or sensitive feet, talk to your veterinarian before starting this work.

• Refer to the photos on pages 50-51 for details on tying up reins and stirrups and on snapping the longe line to the inside bit ring—or, if your horse gets strong or silly, threading the longe line through the inside bit ring and over the poll, snapping it to the outside bit ring.

• Point or raise your whip, slice the air, even bop your horse on the butt if he really tunes you out, but don't do "lion-taming" whip cracks. If you do, some other rider's horse may explode (never appreciated by the rider), and you may teach yours to react to jolts—a lesson you won't appreciate when he hears a candy wrapper crackle during a test and thinks it's a longe whip.

• Time for Lendon's soapbox! I am fanatical about two things: You must hold your longe line with both hands—tracking right, as I am in the photos on pages 53-54, keep one thickness in your right hand and

the leftovers in your left, so you can smoothly shorten and lengthen as well as hang on if your horse takes off. And you must "ribbon" the unused portion across your palm, NOT wrap it around your hand. You can't imagine how easy it is for the best, most wonderful little ol' broke horse in the world to bolt, trap your hand in a coil, and drag you. Why take a chance on injury or death when it's so easy to be safe?

• Keep it interesting! You can do almost everything on the longe that you can under saddle—shortening and lengthening stride, slowing down and speeding up (say "trot slooooooow" or "trot FORWARD"), transitions, spirals in and out.

• Longe for half an hour (or fifteen to twenty minutes before riding) three times a week, and within a month your horse will be suppler and stronger. Change direction at least twice per session (e.g., five minutes to the right, five to the left, five to the right, five to the left). Separate sessions—don't longe three days in a row. And keep him from getting one-sided by alternating your starting direction. (If he resists starting one way, tell him, "This is something you don't do. You don't pick your teeth in public, and you don't refuse to longe to the left first.")

• If you and your horse have never longed, *follow my method to the letter*. If you just slap him in side reins, there's a real risk he'll panic and rear or flip over backward.

Get Equipped

To longe your horse safely, you'll need . . .

• paddock shoes or boots with a heel, but no spurs—they're too easy to trip over as you turn.

• gloves

• your horse in polo wraps or galloping boots, a saddle, and a bridle with a flash or drop noseband, as shown on page 53. If he's the sensitive type, you can add a surcingle to keep your saddle from flapping.

• a cotton longe line with a snap. I don't like a chain unless I'm longeing a bull elephant (which I have done, by the way, but that's another story). A chain tends to make a horse raise his head, and its dead weight interferes with your contact.

• leather side reins with rubber donuts. Elastic side reins are too stretchy and tend to make horses lean; plain side reins are too ungiving and encourage horses to drop behind.

• as long a longe whip as you can comfortably handle

• a longeing area that has a decent surface and a fenced corner.

Start Without Side Reins

Lead your horse out, check his tack, and make any necessary adjustments. Then put him on a 15- to 20-meter circle to the right to gauge whether he's going to be reasonable and give you some control. Keep a fairly straight line from your right elbow to the bit; with your left hand, point the whip toward his hocks. After several walk strides, say "TROT" or "trohut." If he charges off, say "whoa." If he doesn't slow down, say "whoa" and give a sharp snap-release (no hanging, please): the longeing equivalent of a really strong "half-halt idea." This aid may seem a little ugly, but he *must* be obedient; if you have to be rough right now to get that obedience, so be it. He

. . . AND LONGE

1. There's not a lot of body-building value to longeing this way: The side reins are quite loose, Jamboree isn't reaching into the bridle, and there's no connection with my hand. A few simple transitions—trot/walk, walk/trot—might give him a little time and encouragement to stretch; if that doesn't help, I'll stop, walk out to him, and shorten the side reins so he can reach them.

2. Ahhh . . . I've shortened them a couple of holes, and the transitions have helped Jamboree relax, lower his neck, and seek the bit. He isn't pulling or leaning on the side reins—if he were, the donuts would be oval instead of round—but stretching into them, able to reach without feeling restricted in his neck. He's carrying himself, moving forward, freeing up, learning to use the muscles I'll want to sit on. (When a horse's muscles are weak and tight, sitting on his back is like sitting on a board. Jamboree looks more like a couch.) By the way, I don't like this heavy longe line. It's very low to the ground, making soft, conversational contact difficult. *(Continued on next page)*

. . . AND LONGE *(continued)*

3. I've challenged Jamboree with transitions—trot/walk, walk/trot, bigger trot/smaller trot/bigger trot, trot/canter—just as I would under saddle. He's responded with a bigger trot and a better-balanced stride with more self-carriage. Here's the great thing about transitions: If I'd come out and said, "You MUST have power right away," he would have gotten quick, dropped his back, and lifted his head. But because I've taken the time to relax him, he can use himself correctly at a quieter, slower tempo, and he's showing me that he's learning to push off from behind.

4. Wow! This is tracking up to perfection! Jamboree's right hind is about to step dead into the print of his right fore—maybe even a little in front of it. He's a bit on his forehand, and he's come a little close to forging (catching his front foot with the toe of his hind); but as his balance improves, his front foot will get even quicker off the ground and the problem will disappear.

mustn't latch into the idea that he can careen around and ignore you, so do what you need to do to restore a rhythmic, relaxed trot. If he's totally manhandling you, halt, walk out to him, and put the longe line over his poll. Trot again; when he's going quietly, ask him to halt. (Make sure he stops on the track of the circle; you don't want him turning in toward you.)

Once he's halted, walk over to him, ribboning the longe line as you go. Stand beside his head, facing forward. Then, with one rein in each hand, just behind the bit, remind him to give to pressure: Take on one rein to bend him in that direction; let him straighten; then take on the other rein to bend in that direction and let him straighten. As you did from the saddle in Lesson 6, move the bit in his mouth to ask him to come rounder; just play with it so he starts to think, "I remember this. When I give to pressure, the pressure goes away."

LENDON'S CHALLENGE

As you build more power in your trot, do you keep the qualities you MUST have in the beginning: relaxation, rhythm, acceptance of the bit? And can your horse do transitions as well as he does each gait, maintaining balance and self-carriage?

When you feel you've got that point across . . .

Add One Side Rein . . .

. . . to the girth on the outside, adjusting so the side rein is horizontal when your horse's nose is slightly in front of the vertical, slack when his head is straight, and making contact when you turn his nose slightly to the inside. Trot, occasionally pulling on the longe line to turn his head, bring his nose to the inside, and create contact.

When your horse seems OK with this . . .

Add the Other Side Rein . . .

. . . to the girth on the inside, adjusted to the same length as the outside rein. Ask him to go forward again, and see what happens—because from here on, giving to the pressure is something *he has to learn*; beyond what you've already done, you can't teach him. If he hits the side reins and flings his head in the air or starts to run backward, let him go and don't say a word (he won't hear you anyway). If he gets to the end of the longe line, go with him. He'll stop eventually, realize he can't run away from that pressure, and put his head down. When he does, praise him, ask him to walk forward, and trot again.

After five or six trot circles, when you know your horse isn't going to have a temper tantrum . . .

Shorten the Side Reins . . .

. . . to help him start rounding his back and using his topline. (Now, as you walk in and out to adjust and readjust those side reins, you'll realize what a major form of exercise longeing can be for *you*. I've been known to make as many as fifteen adjustments in one session—shortening, testing, evening up,

loosening one, tightening the other. . . .)

Your goal in adjusting the reins is to get your horse traveling straight on the curving track and taking an even pressure on both reins. Most horses will do so when the side reins are the same length; so to start, shorten both reins by two holes. Give him several minutes to settle into the new adjustment. If he takes even pressure and his neck is straight on the curving track, great! But if, like many horses, he's naturally hollow on one side—let's say he bends his neck to the outside (which is typical)—shorten the inside rein an extra hole or two, or more, so his neck is straight or slightly bent to the inside. If he's extremely hollow to the inside, you'll have to shorten the outside rein several holes until the pressure he has on the reins is even.

Remember, don't go by the hole numbers on the side reins. The *effect* is what's important. Whether your horse is hollow to the outside or to the inside, walk out and readjust until it's just right, because "almost good enough" is not acceptable. Adjust, adjust, and readjust; that's the key to success in longeing.

As you work, look for the same relaxation, rhythm, and obedience you seek under saddle. Look for your horse to stay on the track in a soft, even bend—he's not here for exercise now; he's here to develop muscles—with his neck low and his face pretty much on the vertical. Look for a powerful engine pushing from behind and no dawdling or making gullies in the sand. Look for a regular two-beat rhythm. Look for tracking up—his hind foot steps in the print of his same-side forefoot. And look for him not to lean on the reins (he *is* leaning if the rubber donut is an oval instead of a circle—and you need to use your whip to ask him to come more energetically from behind). ■

ON THE LONGE

1. Michele is developing confidence in her ability to grab leather and be OK if her horse trips or runs forward, and getting a sense of real depth, by pulling herself into the saddle with her outside hand. Her leg position is pretty good, but she's experiencing a common problem with this exercise: She's leaning back, tucking her butt, and "waterskiing," rather than sitting squarely on her seat bones. As for me, I wish I weren't using this darned longe line—it's strong, but it's so heavy that I can't maintain a good horizontal line and connection between my hand and Aastrakhan's mouth.

2. In "The Helicopter," Michele is getting the feeling of upper- and lower-body independence by twisting at the waist while keeping her head centered over her chest, her arms out straight (if she were holding a broomstick behind her, it would lie flat against her shoulder blades), and her seat good—she's really sitting squarely on her seat bones. She's a little behind her leg, probably because she's braced against the stirrups; that's not

(Continued on page 58)

LENDON'S CHALLENGE

Can you keep your arms straight and horizontal, so you get the twisting effect at your waist, without losing your lower-leg position?

On the Longe:
Ready, Set, Sit

IN THE LAST TWO LESSONS, WE worked on what your horse needs for sitting trot. In this one, we'll focus again on you.

You absolutely cannot sit the trot if you're stiff or tense, because sitting trot is one of those things you can't *make* yourself do—you can only *allow* it to happen. To make that possible, we're going to put you up on your great new longe partner for three of my favorite loosening, relaxing, suppling exercises:

• The Helicopter—By twisting your upper body, you'll create independence between your torso and seat, and you'll tune in to (and learn to release) any tension you might be holding onto.

• The Wave—By stretching your arms overhead and bending your torso to one side and then the other, you'll relax and release one side of your waist while stretching the other, and so loosen your lower back.

• The Scissors—By "scissoring" your legs, you'll open your hips, increase your thighs' range of motion, and sink your seat into the saddle.

Once you're loose and relaxed, we'll take you off the longe and ease you into sitting trot one stride at a time. And because you're still bound to bounce or lose security, I'll give you some quick-and-easy fixes to help you sit again.

Before You Begin

Let me remind you once again: To longe safely, you must have a helper—a knowl-edgeable friend or a professional—holding the longe line. Longeing is a time-honored learning tool, but it helps only when it's done right. Done wrong, it can be counter-productive, a waste of time, and extremely dangerous. So make sure your longe person can maintain total control over your horse. You're depending on her not just to make him whoa and go, but to prevent him from leaning in or bulging out and to keep him rhythmic and forward. (Your goal is relax-ation, and you can't relax if you're constant-ly kicking to keep him on the circle and moving.)

Above all, you're depending on your helper for your safety: She must know not to let the longe line drag on the ground and must be able to anticipate and prevent bucks, bolts, and scoots. Her job also includes making sure you do the exercises correctly—you're not getting twisted off the saddle one way or the other, your legs are loose when they're supposed to be loose, and your arms are soft and relaxed no mat-ter what "dramatic" moves you're making with your legs.

Now, listen! It is by no means the end of the world if a lack of expert help pre-vents you from doing these exercises on the longe. Still, you must have somebody watch you—and even your Great-Aunt Gertie can tell if you're not sitting straight. Lesson 8's work improved your horsemanship and gave you a valuable technique for creating a stronger, suppler, rounder dressage partner

ON THE LONGE *(continued)*

unusual when your upper and lower body start doing unrelated things. She needs to face forward momentarily and bring her leg back under her—or try the exercise without stirrups so she won't have anything to brace against.

3. In "The Wave," Michele is loosening her back (a necessity for sitting trot) by "letting go" of the right side of her body and stretching out the left. This is purely a suppling exercise for waist and back, so we want to see her stay centered in the saddle, her arms moving only as much as her waist and shoulders do. But she's throwing her hips slightly away from the bend, and her right arm has dropped more than her left; that will give her a false sense that her waist is doing more than it is.

4. The objective of "The Scissors" is for Michele to loosen and increase the mobility of her hip joints, not just swing her lower leg or twist her seat from right to left—so she's pointing her toes, locking her knees, keeping her legs perfectly straight, and holding the pommel to center herself. Even at the trot, she's beautifully balanced and in line.

Inset A: From the side, here's a great forward starting "scissor" position: Michele's leg is about as straight as it can be, her toe pointed as much as a riding boot will allow. Her upper body is well aligned, her seat evenly centered on both seat bones. She happens to have both arms straight out from her shoulders, but that doesn't come right away, especially on a moving horse.

Inset B: This backward finishing position looks great. Michele's thigh is about as far back as it can go, with her knee locked and her toe pointed. Her seat has come a little bit off the saddle—inevitable in the beginning—but with practice she'll be able to bring that leg back while keeping her seat on the saddle and very, very even.

LENDON'S CHALLENGE

Can you scissor your legs while keeping your toes pointed and your knees locked throughout?

who's easier to sit. For *this* lesson you'll simply do the exercises as you've done in the past—on passive contact (you can't, in all fairness, think about your position and your horse's bend) or, if he just trundles along and carries you, on a completely loose rein.

Longeing or not, and even if your horse is Steady Eddie, think twice about using him for this lesson's work if he's sensitive, or if he's enough of a worrier that changes of position or lots of arm- and leg-swinging might make him take off. You can't relax completely if you're worried about him.

Pick a work area with good footing—neither hard nor slippery—in a quiet, uncluttered corner of the ring where there are few distractions and your horse won't have to dodge such obstacles as jump standards or poles on the ground. And before you climb into the saddle for these exercises, longe him to get him warmed up, settled, and accepting the side reins (which you must use to maintain a rhythm and keep him round and soft to sit on). Then tighten your girth (you'd be amazed how many people forget this little detail)—and knot your reins as in the photos on page 50, so they're out of the way but grabbable if needed.

After mounting, reassure yourself that you can manage in an emergency by holding the pommel with your outside hand and pulling yourself deep into the saddle. Don't tuck your butt or lean back—you'll produce a waterskiing-type effect that we don't want.

When you feel comfortable at the walk and the trot, move on to the exercises. Do them in both directions, and ultimately at all three gaits, but introduce each one at the walk—or even, for safety, at the halt, with your longe person standing at your horse's head holding the bridle.

Following the Motion

1. At the moment when she would ordinarily sit in posting the trot, Michele's lower back is in a normal position with a slight curve or arch to it.

2. In the next moment, when she'd ordinarily get bounced out of the saddle and rise, her completely relaxed back and thighs allow her to round and soften her lower back and so absorb the motion.

EASING INTO SITTING

1. Here Michele goes from a slightly forward upper-body position during the rising moment of the posting trot . . .

2. . . . . to that first moment of sitting. Her upper body comes slightly back, she stays in the "down" part of her post, and all her "let go" work on the longe pays off as her loose, open, relaxed lower back and hips allow her to follow her horse. One quibble: She may not have given her hands forward to compensate for her upper-body change—you want to let absolutely nothing happen to your horse's mouth when you go from posting to sitting. However, Aastrakhan can't be too unhappy: Her stride is the same (it hasn't shortened, quickened, or slowed), and her frame and attitude are very nice.

The Helicopter

You'll create independence between your upper and lower body and let go of tension.

Lift your arms straight out to the sides at shoulder height, and twist at the waist to turn your chest and arms to the outside and then to the inside. Keep your seat soft and deep in the saddle, evenly weighted on both seat bones, your legs relaxed and at the girth, and your heels aligned under your hips (and, when facing forward, your ears). To get the full effect of really twisting and loosening your body, swing your arms only as much as your chest turns and NO MORE—you should look as if a broomstick held along the back of your arms would lie flat against your shoulder blades.

The Wave

You'll loosen your back by stretching one side of your waist while you "let go" of the other side.

Lift your arms straight up over your head and bend your upper body sideways,

making sure your legs stay completely relaxed and at the girth, your weight stays evenly balanced on both seat bones, and your arms stay on either side of your head without collapsing or bending more than your torso. Alternate left and right bends.

The Scissors

You'll free up and increase the range of motion of your hip joints. (Please note: This exercise really works your hip joints. Avoid injury by starting slowly and carefully, and stop immediately if you feel pain at any time.)

Remove your stirrups, or cross them over your horse's withers (pull the buckles partway down—see photo 4, inset A, on page 58—so the leathers flatten against the saddle and don't dig into your thighs). Hold the pommel with both hands (later you can hold your inside arm straight out to the side and put just your outside hand on the pommel; eventually you'll put both arms straight out as in "The Helicopter"). Point

your toes like a ballet dancer's and lock your knees so your whole leg—from toe to hip—is completely straight. Try to keep your seat deep in the saddle as you "scissor": Move one leg, from the thigh, forward and the other leg, from the thigh, back (not very far at first, believe me). Hold the position for several beats as you savor the stretch of your hips opening and your seat sinking down before "scissoring" back.

Off the Longe

Pick up your stirrups and ask your horse for an energetic posting trot on about a 20-meter circle. Check your posture to make sure you're carrying your upper body as if you were gliding lightly across the floor—or ring—with your chest lifted and your head up (not slouching along, all heavy and "lumpy"), in the balance and with the poise that will let your seat and legs softly "hang" down around your horse and your lower back swingily follow his motion.

Whether you're on a loose, loopy rein or (as you will be later) on contact, push your hands slightly forward and sit two strides as if to change your posting diagonal. As you do, follow your horse's motion by allowing your lower back to arch a little in the "sitting" moment of the trot, then allowing it to tuck or flatten in the following "rising" moment. After two strides, post again, bringing your hands ever-so-slightly back. In posting, your upper body is a bit more forward than in sitting, so consciously moving your hands forward and back keeps you from inadvertently increasing rein pressure or losing contact.

When you're comfortable and relaxed sitting two strides, increase one stride at a time to three, four, and so on. But never go beyond what you can do without bouncing, falling apart, or losing security, because . . .

You Cannot Sit in Tension

Go back and get yourself comfortable, relaxed, and sitting down and around your horse again—especially if he's reacting to your sitting by making his back tense and hard (he stiffens, you bounce because his back is hard, he gets more tense, you bounce more, et cetera). Break up the cycle of stiffness and resistance by walking and doing leg lifts, cantering partway around the circle to get his back up and relaxed, posting, getting up in jumping position—SOMETHING—until you and he are once again round and relaxed. Then try sitting a few strides again.

If your horse continues to stiffen, tense, or get less fluent, and if you can truthfully say, "I'm not bouncing, gripping, or grabbing him in the mouth" (Great-Aunt Gertie can confirm or deny this fact), his back simply may not be strong or supple enough. In that case, he needs more longe and hill work. ■

WALKING OVER THE CAVALLETTI

Before approaching this ground pole, my student Erica Hogg (who's a professional hunter trainer) established a balanced two-point position at the walk on the flat. Now everything—loose rein, eyes well ahead, heel down and directly under her hip, hands resting partway up Tab's neck to stabilize her upper body, and seat lightly and easily "rolled" out of the saddle—encourages him to stay relaxed and change nothing as he walks comfortably over the single pole (flat on the ground between two supports at this early stage). Notice (inset) that she's able to maintain an effective, balanced two-point in a dressage saddle with what I call an "all-purpose" stirrup length: a hole or two shorter than for straight dressage, a hole or two longer than for true jumping.

LENDON'S CHALLENGE

Do you use the ball of your foot as your base of support in jumping position, just as you would standing on the ground with your knees slightly bent? If so, you're not making the mistake of gripping with your knee and depending on your seat for support.

Cavalletti

ARE YOU UP FOR SOME FUN? AFTER three lessons concentrating on one of the longest-term projects of dressage—the sitting trot—I say it's time for a BIG change of pace.

Let's face it: Trundling around the ring and focusing on your seat may be critically important to your riding, but it is not the most stimulating thing in the world. So let's bring a change of pace and a huge schpritz of zest to your dressage life by doing something completely different: working over cavalletti (low wooden poles stabilized by stands or blocks).

I'll tell you what kind of equipment you'll need, and how much (cavalletti come in a variety of designs you can buy, build, or improvise), and where and how to set it up. I'll talk about tack (with—yes—another soapbox lecture, this one on stirrup length), how to get started safely and soundly, how to go with your horse and not interfere with him, and how to increase variety and difficulty. Finally, I'll give you an all-purpose cavalletti workout to fold into your regular schooling sessions.

TROTTING THE CAVALLETTI IN TWO-POINT

At the trot, you can see why cavalletti are such a challenge to a rider's balance: With everything so accentuated, from his speed to his bounce, Tab's testing the shock-absorbing capability of Erica's joints to the maximum. How's it going? Her upper body is (as it should be) slightly more forward than at the walk, her leg is under her, her stabilizing hand is barely resting on his neck, and her exaggeratedly loose rein plus his obvious ability to maintain a steady stride and tempo tell us that her ankle, knee, and hip are absorbing his bounce, letting her follow his motion in perfect balance.

Cavalletti

TWO COMMON POSITION PROBLEMS

1. Trying to get her heel down, Erica has pushed her foot forward and braced it, sending her seat backward a little; she no longer has a direct vertical line from hip to heel. Her stirrup may be more on her toe than on the ball of her foot, and I'm pretty certain she's gripping with her calf. She has kept her hands well forward—but if Tab makes any kind of unusual move, she'll plop back into the saddle and jerk on the reins. The best fix for this dilemma is to lighten her heel, letting it act as a bouncy shock-absorber, and push it toward his rear feet.

2. Here a pinching knee blocks her weight from going through into her heel and makes her lower leg float back. As unbalanced as she is, it's a good thing her hands are resting on Tab's neck; if he stumbled, she'd pitch forward. How to get out of this mess? By turning her knee out slightly to "unglue" it, then bringing her foot forward and her upper body back until she's correctly realigned.

We'll continue in this change-of-pace vein in Lesson 11 by getting you completely out of the artificial environment of the arena and onto the trail. Yes, I know you did strengthening and suppling on the trail, but now I'm talking "go for the gusto"—fun, recreation, a little bit of yahoo, and a lot of figuring out your and your horse's balance through a range of good and bad moments, as well as opening the door to what may be your first extended trot. In Lesson 12 we'll add lateral trail work: leg-yielding around holes and opening and closing a gate—useful skills that also serve as a terrific reality check of all your aids and all his training.

In the meantime, if you know me, you know that . . .

Cavalletti Are More Than Fun

Done correctly (I'll tell you how), cavalletti *gymnasticize* your horse by requiring him to raise his feet a bit higher than normal, which helps him to . . .

- strengthen and loosen his muscles
- increase the bend and use of his joints
- adjust his center of gravity
- improve his balance
- develop a rhythm
- arch and round his back
- and maybe, almost as a gift if you're lucky, come on the bit, although that is not necessarily our goal.

At the same time, cavalletti help *you* to . . .

- improve your balance
- deepen your weight in your heel
- increase your confidence and *joie de vivre*
- and go *with* your horse, not against him, as he makes bigger, bouncier moves to clear the cavalletti.

What You'll Need

To do cavalletti successfully, you'll need some new equipment and a skill you've been working on:

1. Six to eight thick wooden poles, heavy and hard enough not to scatter or splinter if your horse accidentally knocks or steps on them. Later, when you raise the poles about 3 inches off the ground, you'll need to stabilize them with four-by-fours or six-by-sixes notched to cradle them, or bolted to them—or with commercially available supports.

2. A helper on the ground—not necessarily a dressage expert, but someone who can adjust, move, and reposition the poles. (Having to get off and on to do this yourself is a major pain—mostly because you don't want to bother. So you're likely to be tempted to start settling for unsuitable distances or poles that are just a little crooked, which is never a good solution.) This helper should also be able to scold you (nicely, of course) about faults that the cavalletti may exaggerate, such as tipping forward over your knees, falling back, or catching your horse in the mouth.

3. Properly adjusted stirrups. Way back in Lesson 1, I mentioned my pet peeve about people who think dressage automatically means long stirrups—and who end up riding with no base of support. But as bad as too-long stirrups are for dressage, they're absolutely *disastrous* for hacking, jumping, and—yes—cavalletti: If your stirrups are even slightly too long and your horse takes a bad step or adds a bit of bounce to his stride, you're going to lose your balance and slam into his back or jerk on his mouth. So adjust your stirrups to what I call an "all-purpose" length—a hole or two shorter than for dressage and a hole or two longer than absolute jumping length. Then, while you warm up, establish . . .

Cavalletti

POSTING THROUGH THE CAVALLETTI

1. Wow! Talk about the gymnastic value of cavalletti, and why posting can be harder than two-point! Here, in the "rise" phase, Tab's motion is really exaggerated as he lifts his feet higher, rounds his back, and bends his joints. If Erica doesn't stay absolutely in balance, she'll really get thrown off (particularly now that she no longer has that little bit of support from resting her hands on his neck and that little bit of slack from the loose rein). She looks great, though—relaxed, balanced over her leg, eyes well ahead, a perfectly straight line from elbow to mouth, upper body slightly forward to accommodate Tab's forward balance. He's responding by coming a little on the bit and accepting her contact. (The contact may actually be a little strong, but that's OK here. Tab tends by nature to seek too much contact, and he's clearly happy in his work.)

4. Two-point position. (Don't bother attempting two-point over cavalletti if you can't maintain two-point on the flat.) Sit with shoulder, hip, and heel lined up; the ball of your foot on the stirrup iron; the stirrup leather on or slightly behind the vertical; and a little depth in your heel and a soft angle behind your knee, as if you were standing on the ground with your knees bent. Then rest (don't push) your hands about a third of the way up your horse's neck and, without gripping your knee or thigh or tightening your back, roll your seat forward out of the saddle. If your stirrups are the right length and your position is correct, you'll balance there, comfortable and secure, as if you could stay forever. If you have trouble getting your weight down, or if you grip with your knees, you

wobble, or anything hurts (other than the stretched-out back of your calf or ankle), sit, relax, realign, and try again.

"Wait," you tell me. "I may feel balanced, but I don't feel very effective." Well, another of the great life lessons I learned from then USET three-day coach Jack Le Goff happened when he had us do a full one-hour session of Third Level dressage—half-passes, simple changes, extensions, walk pirouettes—in two-point. That enlightening experience taught me it's utter garbage to say you can't do stuff without sitting deep. You may not perform at your show-ring best; but as long as your horse is reasonably responsive, you should be able to walk, trot, canter, halt, steer, and do a little leg-yield or anything else we've worked on up to this point. Try it! You'll

LENDON'S CHALLENGE

When you trot through/over the cavalletti, do you maintain exactly the same balance you had while trotting around the ring? Nothing should change.

add a whole new dimension to riding and coordinating your aids.

Start With a Single Pole . . .

. . . in the middle of the ring, so you can alternate directions. At the walk, turn toward the pole. At least four or five strides out, establish your two-point, a loose rein (so you don't accidentally bop your horse if he takes a different step figuring things out), a straight line to the middle of the pole, and any other quality you want *over* the pole—because a major goal of cavalletti work is to keep everything so much the same that you basically look as if you're not doing cavalletti work at all.

Let your horse look at the pole as you approach (if he hesitates or veers off, use leg and voice aids to encourage him forward); maintain everything—position, stride, tempo, line—as he steps over and for four or five strides after. Turn right or left, sit, trot, canter, do whatever you want that's different; then come back around, establish everything four or five strides out, and walk the pole again.

When the pole feels so right, rhythmic, and the same that you and your horse are almost getting bored, do it in posting trot (a little more stable than two-point while you're both getting the feel and rhythm), keeping your balance, depth of weight in your heel, and passive contact exactly the same. The fact that you're trotting changes nothing. Yes, your body has to adapt as he raises his legs higher and emphasizes his rhythm, but that's what your shock-absorbing "springs"—ankle, knee, and hip—are for.

2. This moment of the "sit" phase illustrates the relaxed, solid consistency that Erica and Tab are starting to develop through cavalletti work. Her hips are still over her heels (her foot may be a tiny bit in front, but nowhere near enough to interfere with his way of going), she's looking well ahead, and she still has that nice, direct elbow-to-mouth line. Tab may be a little on the muscle, but he clearly *is* on the aids. I think he's just showing youthful enthusiasm for the fun new game he's learned.

As soon as you're comfortable and confident rising, go to two-point, again establishing your position four or five strides out so you don't jump up on your horse's neck as he's about to step over the cavalletti. If the exercise makes you bounce, imagine I've scattered a box of thumbtacks—point up—on your saddle. No matter what, you don't want to sit on those tacks! (If your seat does hit the saddle anyway, or if your toes point down or your heels won't drop, recheck your stirrups—they may still be too long.)

When your horse maintains a straight line and a confident, happy rhythm to the single pole . . .

> **"If going over a cavalletti in two-point makes you bounce, imagine I've scattered a box of thumbtacks—point up—on your saddle."**

Add Another Pole . . .

. . . about 8 feet from the first, for a normal double trot distance that should discourage him from solving this new arrangement by trying to jump the two. Then walk the two poles in two-point. He'll have to fumble his way through because of the trot striding, but he'll still get the idea that this is no big deal, he can figure it out, and it isn't something to avoid or jump or crash through. When he's relaxed at the walk, trot the two poles in two-point (if the striding doesn't fit, have your helper move the poles in or out until it does), remembering to establish everything—line, position, loose rein, rhythm, and tempo—four or five strides ahead and maintain it to four or five strides after.

When your horse does two poles confidently . . .

Add a Third Pole . . .

. . . between the two (single distance to single distance), or after the two (double to single). Which setup will work for your horse? Good question. If he seems perfectly relaxed with the whole operation, put the pole in the middle. If he tends to rev up or feels as if he wants to jump, put it after, so he's well into the cavalletti rhythm before he comes to the closer, more jumpable set of poles. When the three poles are ho-hum, add three to five more at normal single distances. When he trots *them* without speeding up, slowing down, or trying to run out, pat him. You've done enough for this session.

Next time, raise the poles to about 3 inches off the ground—a good gymnastic height, with a bit more emphasis and only a little more challenge—and keep the line set up inside or alongside your arena for what I call . . .

The Ultimate Cavalletti Session

Warm up your horse with all the elements of a normal schooling session: walk, trot, canter, circles, changes of direction. Then move on to cavalletti—not by saying, "OK, now we are going to do cavalletti forty-two times," but by casually getting up in two-point and trotting the line twice. Come back and maybe work on sitting trot (you can always use more of that, right?) and canter; then trot the cavalletti twice in the other direction. Work circles, transitions, and halts; then trot the cavalletti a couple of times more. Your goal: to make cavalletti a way of life, rather than a big deal, by easily folding them into a regular schooling session and maintaining the same balance, aids, and look, whether you're trotting them or not.

Got it? Great! Have a ball! ■

LESSON 11

Into the
Woods

CONTINUING OUR THREE-PART MINI-vacation from ring work, in this lesson we're going out on the trail. (I know, in Lesson 7 I had you trot your horse up a low hill, but that was a strengthening and suppling dressage exercise with a dash of fun. Now, though, I'm talking fun and recreation with a splash of dressage.) As you wander hill and dale, you'll . . .

• learn to trust in yourself and know what you can deal with—be it difficult foot-ing, low obstacles, or bogeymen in the bushes

• figure out (and improve) your and your horse's balance by negotiating a range of good and bad moments

• naturally experience your first extended trot as your horse pushes uphill with power rather than speed.

Hey, Wait a Minute!

Is that you muttering, "Uh-oh," quietly put-

DOWNHILL

1. What a pleasant, balanced picture! Erica has a soft contact and a fairly direct line from elbow to bit. She's staying clear of the saddle by supporting her weight on the stirrup, freeing Lindekrona to round his back, bend his joints, and step well under himself.

LENDON'S CHALLENGE

Can you ride downhill balanced over your leg, maintaining the same contact on your horse's mouth and keeping your seat completely free of his back?

1

DOWNHILL
(continued)

2. A much less comfortable way to go downhill. Lindekrona is a little above the bit, hollow in his back, and stiff—and look how much straighter and less under him his hind legs are! Erica's stiff, too, but I don't think it's her fault. Lindekrona's doing it incorrectly.

ting down this book, and tiptoeing toward the door? Are you one of those " hothouse flower" riders who never sets foot outside the ring, or who ventures only far enough to get a job done? At my place, for example, would you be the student trotting the manicured hill next to my indoor arena, rather than venturing forth in search of hills—and thrills—unknown? Well, my friend, by not getting out on the trail, exploring the woods, and coping with varied terrains, footings, and circumstances, you and your horse are not only missing wonderful riding, but you're denying yourself a great opportunity to . . .

• learn survival techniques that give you tools and confidence to cope when things aren't absolutely perfect—for example, at shows, where I guarantee warm-up

areas won't always be quiet, empty, spacious, and absolutely level. And some chilly morning your horse is going to buck and get strong. Or he's going to spook at the unexpected: a chicken wandering through the arena, the judge "lurking" inside a horse trailer, or swarms of miniature horses pulling carts. (Believe me, I've dealt with all of those and more.)

• add an extra dimension to your and his adaptability, "negotiability," and athleticism by learning how to adjust (and improve) your balance through a never-ending variety of footings, obstacles, ups, downs, and conditions.

• develop a deeper understanding of him by observing and dealing with his reactions to "impromptu" situations—such as a creek across the trail, tree-trimmers over-

2

head, or dogs barking behind a fence.

• become more tuned in to how his body works. (All his movements are exaggerated when he steps high over a log, pops up a bank, jumps a ditch—you don't, by the way, have to know how to jump to do that—or tucks his butt to slip-slide down a bank.)

• most important of all, have a good time! This is the stuff that keeps you alive and exhilarated about life and dressage. (Let's face it: Ring work can get awfully boring.) In fact, I'm convinced that much of my success inside the arena is a direct result of a childhood spent *outside*, racing around bareback, getting run away with, falling off, and learning—through all of it—how to survive.

Realistically, though, I was a kid. If you're forty, or even twenty, and new to dressage, I am the last person to suggest you need to get frightened or bucked off to learn a life lesson. Quite the contrary: I believe that hacking is fun and productive only when you . . .

Keep Yourself Safe

So follow these guidelines:
1. Start in the company of an experienced, knowledgeable, reassuring, patient rider on a confident, capable, "trail-wise" horse.
2. Head for the trail after a lesson or schooling session, when you and your horse are settled and tuned in to each other—and when he's just tired enough to take things as they come. Eventually you'll be able to do straight ring work some days; head right out and hack some days

LENDON'S CHALLENGE

Can you pop up or down a little bank keeping your center of balance over your horse's, so he has complete freedom to use his head and neck and back?

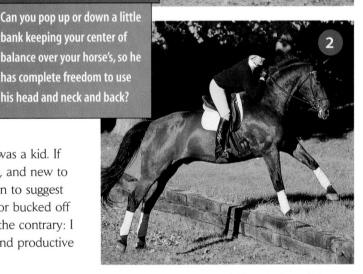

JUMPING UP AND DOWN A BANK

1. Erica doesn't need jumping lessons (and neither do you) to give her horse the complete freedom of back and mouth he needs to pop out of my dressage ring. She's clear of the saddle; her hands are resting well up Lindekrona's neck for support and security; she's staying with his motion—and because she's not interfering . . .

2. . . . . he's able to stick his nose out, use his neck, and go for it.

3. Erica is basically in line, but I'd like her to bring her leg a bit more forward and rest her hands a little farther up the neck for support. She isn't interfering with her horse's mouth or banging him in the back, though, and you just know she's not going to fall behind when he lands and canters away.

THE DITCH: DOWN, ACROSS, AND UP

1. I like Erica's "defensive" position because you never know what's going to happen when a horse sees a little ditch like this. He could slam on the brakes or shoot up in the air like a pogo stick—and if she were in a perfect little two-point, she could get bounced off. Instead, her hands are well forward but resting securely on the crest, she's sitting down and using a bit of a driving seat, and she's maintaining a close, encouraging leg.

2. Erica's taken a good grip on a hunk of mane to keep herself from getting left behind and inadvertently punishing Lindekrona if he jumps awkwardly. She's also off his back, looking to the other side, and keeping her hands well forward to give him a very loose rein. He's making a nice effort.

3. Erica's upper body may be a little too far forward as her horse continues up the bank, but she's staying with him and giving him all the freedom he needs to get there.

(recess time!); and some days do half a session of ring work, then use a fairly straight road to practice transitions or steering with your legs and weight, or use hills and valleys to strengthen, supple, and test and build balance.

3. Adjust your stirrups to "all-purpose" length—a hole or two shorter than for dressage and a hole or two longer than for jumping—to keep your center of gravity over your horse's (I'll tell you how in a moment), and grab a bit of mane for security. God put the mane there to provide a handhold when the footing's unpredictable—and let me tell you, many's the time I've whispered a heartfelt "Thank you, God!"

4. Realize that this isn't about everything being perfect. It's about developing a seat-of-your-pants feel for the relaxation and fluidity you need to go with your horse by quickly and smoothly adjusting your balance.

5. Take baby steps. Your first major accomplishment can be as non-threatening as a walk around the outside of the fence. Next time, go a little farther afield—maybe down the driveway or around the block. Then go down to the bridge, or try popping over a half-buried log, and so on. Challenge yourself, but only within the limits of your comfort zone.

Start Walking Uphill and Downhill

Uphill, you want your horse to push energetically from behind—that's impulsion—and not go faster. Downhill, you want him to shift his weight rearward and keep it there so he doesn't go faster—that's carrying. But pushing and carrying are hard work, especially if he isn't very strong. He may try to make things easier by trotting when he should walk, or cantering when he should trot. Help him push and carry by . . .

• riding up and down hills in two-point, so your balance is over his balance and his rear engine is free to do its work. Place the balls of your feet on the stirrup irons; going uphill, rest your hands about a third of the way up his neck (remember to grab a bit of mane—or, if you feel insecure, buckle a stirrup leather around his neck and hold that). Push down on the balls of your feet and drive your weight into your heels, emphasizing that downward push with every stride; and—without gripping your calves, knees, or thighs, or tightening your back—roll your seat forward out of the saddle. On uphills and basic downhills, keep your heels and hips aligned but bring your shoulders forward; on steep downhills, keep all three aligned by pushing your feet forward and bringing your shoulders back. You'll know you're right when you feel as if you could stay there forever, whether you're powering up the side of a mountain or slithering down a tiny slope.

• riding on contact (at least in the beginning) so you can "shortstop" your horse's attempts to switch to a higher gait or speed.

• riding straight down hills so he steps under his body, holds himself back, and is less likely (should he slip) to fall sideways and more likely to sit safely down.

When you feel solid and secure at the walk and your horse feels balanced and straight and consistent, seek out a slight up-and-down place, such as a ridge, hump, or swale, and . . .

Trot Up and Down

Going up, look for a change in oomph—even a little bit of extended trot, which should feel like a surge of power, a longer stride, and a hesitating moment of suspension between steps. When you get to the top of the rise and begin your turn, use a "half-halt idea" (see Lesson 5) to help your horse slow, shift his weight back, and prepare himself to hold and carry as he trots back down: Squeeze your "inside" leg at the girth, soften him slightly with your "inside" rein so he doesn't brace against your hand, and then momentarily bring both elbows back to pull or tug on the reins. If gravity takes over, say "whoa" and ask him to walk and reorganize, then trot on—because trotting in balance down even a tiny dip can be extremely difficult for a young or weak horse, but it's the best way to build his strength and balance.

How Much Should Your Horse Do?

At my place, young horses who have iffy balance or weak stifles get regular hill work twice a week; older horses do random hills on their weekly hacks. Listen to your horse. Check his breathing and feel how hard he's working. When he's comfortably doing what you ask, add more; when he struggles, takes a long time to recover, or starts telling you where you can go with your darned hills, ease off. (Don't be *too* easy on him, though, because if he never gets a little tired, he'll never build himself up.)

And remember: Trail-riding is supposed to be fun! If you're in Colorado, go climb a low mountain. If you're in Arizona, explore the desert. If you're at Claremont Riding Academy in New York City, go to Central Park; then get off the bridle trails. Scramble through streams. Climb banks. Wander down side roads. Jump logs. Have some carefree times enjoying the great outdoors with your horse. That's what he—and this big country—are here for. ■

WORKING THE GATE

How's this for a change of career? Lindekrona has won US Dressage Federation Regional Championships at most levels through Intermediaire II—but the way he works this gate, he's got a great future as a ranch horse, even though he's a little spooky and uncertain starting out! Erica's right leg is back, pressing, asking him to leg-yield toward the gate so he'll end up parallel to it, with his haunches toward the hinge and his head toward the latch. She's keeping him bent away from the direction he's going—not only the correct way to leg-yield (and a good way to keep him from sticking his head over the gate), but the best way to keep his mind on his work and off the spooky "monster." Her right rein is firmly against his neck, and what I can see of her left arm tells me she's using an inviting open left rein. If I had a nit to pick, it would be that her right hand is a little raised and she appears to be leaning back.

2. Having arrived next to the gate, with Erica well within reach of the latch—and despite his mild but continued uncertainty about this strange creature next to him—Lindekrona gives a great demonstration of what I call "stabilization": his willingness to pause, stand still, and obediently wait for what comes next. Erica's certainly doing her best to reassure him as she reaches to undo the latch. Her right leg is still against his side, so he knows he's not to step away; her left leg is comfortingly close; and without pulling back, she's maintaining a soft but definite rein contact.

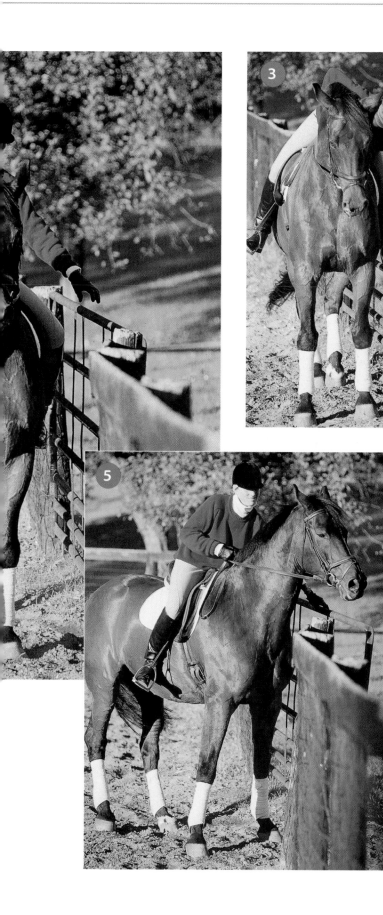

3. This moment can be dangerous: Erica could really get into trouble if she leaned too far down, pulled on the reins and made Lindekrona back up and resist, or let her right heel come off his side and float up toward the saddle pad (which would tell him to move away just when it's essential that he stay there). Fortunately, even as she fumbles with the catch, she's got a very good sense of where her legs are—close without clutching—and her base is good and solid, with plenty of weight in both heels. She also has a good feel for what I call "her brain in her hand": a very nice rein contact that's just enough "there" to reassure him. (If she had trouble with the latch, I'd have her play it safe and dismount to fiddle with it.)

4. Talk about independence of aids! As Erica asks Lindekrona to move his forehand one small step to the left (it has to move farther than his haunches because the gate's "handle" end swings on a bigger arc than the hinge end), her left hand controls the gate. Her right hand presses the right rein against his neck, asking him to move his forehand over, and makes sure the reins stay even so he doesn't turn his head to the right. (He has to stay between two reins, whether she's holding them in one hand or two.) She's pressing her right leg at the girth to ask him to move his forehand more (compare with the first photo, where she was asking him to move forehand and haunches together). And even though she is of necessity leaning left, her feet are level: She's consciously stepping more heavily into her right heel to counteract her leftward tilt. I'm impressed that Lindekrona's head is low; he looks soft and trusting and quiet and settled.

5. Whoops! His forehand has gone left, but he's moved his haunches right, putting Erica in a bit of an awkward position and forcing her to slide her hand along the top of the gate just to hang on. Most people fall apart and

WORKING THE GATE *(continued)*

lose the gate at this point because they can't say, "Wait just a minute. Whoa. Let's think about this and not do anything until I say so." But Erica—and this is where the "stabilization" is so important—took a soft, soft contact with her right hand to tell him to go nowhere, and he paused and allowed her to regroup quietly (a great test of her aids and his training). Now, with her right leg considerably behind the girth, she's telling him to move his haunches back to the left, where they belong.

6. Erica's now pushed the gate open far enough to start walking slowly forward, one step at a time. She really has Lindekrona on the aids: Her even right-hand contact is containing him, saying, "Just a little bit, just a little bit." Her right leg is back in very close contact, making sure he doesn't swing or spin his haunches around and hit the post. Her slightly forward left leg is telling him just how much to go ahead. Her left hand is still holding and pushing the gate. And even though she's leaning over, she's balanced and not pulling him. Talk about patting your head and rubbing your tummy: Each part of her body has a different job, and they're all working together! She'll continue walking forward, one half-step at a time . . .

7. . . . until there's plenty of room for Lindekrona's right hip to fit past the post and start a step-by-step turn on the forehand off her left leg (his left hind is just lifting and getting ready to cross over).

Apparently they aren't quite through the gate; she can use half-steps to adjust his stride, literally one step at a time, so he . . .

8. . . . goes sideways a step, forward another step, and sideways another step until they're through.

9. Lindekrona's come completely around. In the next moment, Erica will start to close the gate. Once again, she could lose it because he has to go from moving his hind end sideways to moving sideways and back to get her close to the fence post. She keeps her right hand centered on his crest, presses the right rein against his neck to ask him to move his shoulders left and . . .

10. . . . slightly back with each step (look how he's listening), until, in a very organized, step-by-step process . . .

11. . . . she's closed the gate and is next to the post, where she can redo the latch. (Again, if she has trouble doing so, she should dismount—and not tempt fate.) ■

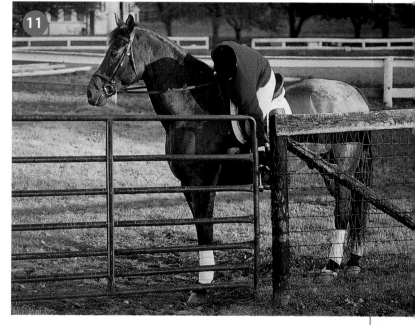

Put Him On the Aids

WELCOME BACK FROM YOUR MINI-vacation! I hope you and your horse are feeling invigorated from learning new skills. He's probably mentally refreshed, rounder, and more forward-thinking; you're probably more balanced, stronger, more independent of seat and aids, more able to ride without hanging, and more aware of how much contact you feel—all of which will help you ride him on the bit.

I'm not calling this lesson "Put Him on the Bit," though, because "on the bit" could tempt you to focus on creating a "head set," with your horse's face on the vertical, and little else. "On the aids" conveys the whole picture: He's coming from your leg, stepping toward the bit, and yielding to your hand in a fluid, soft, elastic way while he continues to move forward. "On the aids" conveys *throughness*—a quality I describe to my students as "squishability." When you sit deep and close your leg and your fingers (or take back slightly), your horse responds with total willingness. Keeping a smooth, consistent rhythm, he steps forward, yields his jaw, and "comes together," with no resistance anywhere. He's even in both reins; he bends evenly in both directions. At any moment, he can shorten up and squish his frame together or stretch and make it longer.

He May Already Be on the Bit

There's a good chance that, as you've worked your way through the previous les-

sons, your horse may automatically have started yielding both sides of his jaw at once, flexing at the poll, and coming rounder. In Lesson 6, for example, "walking the square" helped you connect his front end to his hind end, place him between your inside leg and outside rein, and bend his body as well as his neck; and "vibrating the bit" made the bit come alive in his mouth and encouraged him to give at the poll. If your horse still isn't flexing and coming round, he may be bracing and holding one side of the bit. Why would he do that? For any number of reasons, the most likely

HE CAN BEND

Near left: If your horse doesn't bend, it's probably not because he's stiff. Like my student Erin Collins's Regal, seen here, he may well be in the habit of bracing against his rider's hand—and may need to learn to answer your rein aid. (Regal, a thirteen-year-old Morgan, competed in park harness and saddle-seat divisions until he was nine. Among the things we're working on is his tendency either to go right against the bit like this or to come behind the vertical.)

Opposite: Here's the proof that Regal isn't stiff. The carrot in my hand has convinced him to bring his neck around and show how incredibly supple he truly is.

TRAINING AIDS: LIFTING THE BIT AND COUNTER-BENDING

1. A horse that braces may be less resistant to your bending aid if you raise your hand straight up and place the bit in the corner of his lip, rather than on the bars of his mouth (his gums). This is a training aid, not something you'll do forever.

2. Bending a resistant horse in one direction and getting him to give one side of his jaw, then in the other direction and getting him to give the other side, encourages him to come on the bit. On a circle to the right, Regal is softly bending and giving his jaw to the outside. He's come a little behind the vertical, not a major sin right now—but Erin should be shot for not looking where she's going!

being that he bends more easily in one direction than the other (most horses do), or that he's compensating for a physical weakness, lameness, injury, or even for the effects of a previous rider with one Godzilla arm. Whatever the reason (other than lameness or injury; have your veterinarian rule these out if his resistance persists), the exer-

cises in this lesson—bending him toward his harder side on a 20-meter circle, and changing the bend from one side to the other on a figure eight—should help him.

If your horse is already on the bit, do these exercises anyway—the circle is a terrific check of your aids, and the figure eight is a, classic confirmation that he's even in both reins and bending equally in both directions. If he remains braced and resistant *after* this lesson, check out "If Your Horse Still Braces" on page 85.

You'll Succeed If You . . .

• Identify your horse's easy or "hollow" side and his "hard" side. (Don't call it "stiff"—"stiff" is what we get when we're old. Moreover, the problem isn't that he can't bend; it's that he doesn't answer your hand.) Here are two ways to tell which side is which: First, trot him on a loose rein on a straight line. You'll feel or see him hollow or bend more in one direction; that's his "hollow" side. Second, ask him to bend to one side and then to the other. The side that feels "too easy" is his hollow side.

• Take plenty of breaks. *As soon as you have success, quit for the day*, because this is hard work for your horse.

• Know the difference between "on the aids," in which your horse comes from your leg, steps toward the bit, and yields to your hand, and a "head set," in which he feels unable or unwilling to respond when you ask him to come rounder, raise or lower his neck, or stretch his neck and nose out in front.

• Don't sweat the transitions. Even as your horse starts to stay nicely round at the walk and trot, he's probably going to root (snatch downward) or come above the bit in his transitions. If you fight him or try to keep him round, you'll set up a resistance that will destroy everything you've accom-

ON THE AIDS THROUGH A FIGURE EIGHT

1. Regal is softly bending to the right, moving forward decently, with no resistance—and that's what makes a circle a circle. Erin's inside leg could be closer to the girth—but when your horse is small for you, keeping your leg at the girth is harder.

2. At the halfway point between bending right and bending left, there should be a moment of straightness when your horse is even between both legs and both reins. Regal is moving nicely straight ahead, his nose centered over his chest.

3. A moment later, Erin asks him for the left bend with her left leg at the girth and her left rein, and follows with her right rein to allow him to go in the new direction. Her right calf is still on; it should be back a little more.

4. Now her right leg is better, and she has a nice, soft connection in the rein. Regal's giving the appearance of bending pretty much the same in both directions: a soft right bend, one stride of straightness, and then a nice left bend. That's what we want. And Erin's looking up!

LENDON'S CHALLENGE

Can you change the bend within two strides while your horse keeps everything the same—staying on the aids, not coming above the bit, maintaining his frame and rhythm, and bending equally and easily to left and right?

TEST YOUR BENDING

As Erin gives up the inside rein for a stride or two, Regal maintains his soft bend, proving she's not holding his head in position. I'd like more bend and less flexion, but he *is* showing he can keep his head quiet and stay on the outside rein without counterbending. Do this exercise on a smaller circle with more bend, too.

plished. Just maintain passive contact, let him do whatever he's going to do, reestablish a good rhythm in the new gait, ask him to come round, and enjoy.

On the Aids on a Circle

Pick up an energetic, marching walk in the direction of your horse's harder side—let's say it's the right. Then, with your inside leg at the girth and your outside leg behind the girth to maintain the arc of the circle, ask him to bend to the inside for two or three strides; take just enough steady, slight leading rein—a little back and to the inside—that he gives and softens his jaw without turning right. Don't jerk; just pull steadily until he gives. You may have to raise your hand to

place the bit in the corner of his lip, where he can't brace against you. You may have to pull with all your might. You may have to be very strong—but if you must, you must, until he softens and gives.

Now, don't get so focused on the right rein that you let the left rein drop or float. "On the aids" means we are looking for your horse to end up the same in *both* reins, so you want—you need—him to find the contact and connection on the left, not with a pulling but with a light quality of "thereness." You may even want to leg-yield him out on the circle a step or two; *that* gets him to step away from the inside rein and creates the sense of pushing him toward the left rein so he "takes" it and fills it out. That left rein becomes a soft "wall," preventing him from falling out. (Ultimately, when you put your inside leg on, he won't actually go sideways. He'll just give you the sense of energy surging toward the outside rein.)

When your horse finally does give his jaw, soften, and bend to the right (the muscles on the inside of his neck will go from bulging to concave, and you'll feel a lightness in your right hand), allow the left side of his mouth to take your left hand forward; simultaneously, soften your right hand. He'll probably stay bent for two or three strides; then, as a reward, allow him to straighten for two or three strides. Occasionally—to remind him, "See how easy this can be"—counterbend him to the outside for two or three strides. Straighten him

LENDON'S CHALLENGE

See if your horse will maintain the bend on a 20-meter circle to his harder side when you have *no* inside rein. Go on, give it forward!

again; then go back to his hard side.

As your horse relaxes his hard side through this stretching and becomes more even in both reins, he'll naturally start to come round. When he does, resist the temptation to try to hold him there. Instead, immediately stop asking, let him stretch his nose out and his neck down, and say, "Thank you very much." Gradually, he'll learn to maintain the roundness longer. In the meanwhile, he won't be perfect any more than I'd be ambidextrous after writing one word with my left hand, but he'll be *better*. When that happens on the circle, try . . .

On the Aids Through a Figure Eight

. . . of two 20-meter circles. Doing this will confirm that your horse can smoothly go from bend to bend, leg to leg, and rein to rein, and stay pretty equal and even: a perfect recipe, and almost a perfect definition, for "on the bit."

Pick up a forward posting trot on a 20-meter circle to your horse's harder side—let's say the right again. As you approach the "X" point where the two circles touch, change his bend to the left. Press your left leg on the girth to bend him toward the right rein, and allow your right hand to "stretch" with his new outside as your left hand "suggests" a little bend to his new inside—the easy or hollow left. In this direction, the bend will probably happen easily and maintain itself.

At the X point, you'll go back to your horse's harder side again. The issue here: You want him to answer immediately and equally—not after half a circle's worth of wearing him down, not bracing or coming above the bit, and not with any less bend than he gave you on his hollow side. Use a stronger right hand to "suggest/demand" the right bend emphatically, and a stronger right leg at the girth—you'll have to experiment with how much—to encourage him to give the right side of his body, jaw, and neck, stay out on the circle, and push himself toward his new outside left rein. It should almost go like this: "Bend, please. . . . Thank you." You have to be able to immediately soften him, then not hold him, for him to bend correctly around your inside leg, creating the new connection and filling up the outside rein. ■

If Your Horse Still Braces

. . . you can try the following:

• Make the bit "alive" in his mouth by sliding it left and right on his tongue, without backward pressure, as explained in Lesson 6.

• Don't get into a tug of war. Give on the inside rein, ask, and give again. At the moment you give, when he has nothing to brace against, he may momentarily soften. If, in that instant, you sneak in and ask again, he may just give to you.

• Bend him with a firm inside hand, keep your inside leg at the girth, and give and take with the outside rein. Then, whether he flexes and gives or continues to brace, give to him immediately. As you've already learned, if you hang, he just hangs back.

Remember, though, that what you practice is what your horse learns--so *if it ain't workin', stop doin' it!* After five or six unsuccessful requests, walk forward on a loose rein and reevaluate. This may be the point at which you must get professional help or you'll just keep teaching him to brace, resist, tune you out, and ignore your aids.

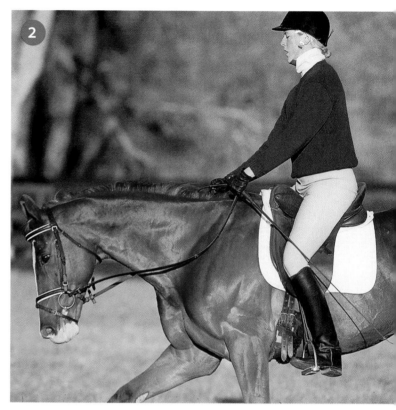

TEACHING THE STRETCH

1. To begin, Erin "megabends" six-year-old Cohiba, raising her inside hand so that the bit comes against the most effective spot—his sensitive lips. She's intentionally using too-long reins to be sure she'll be able to give enough when he stretches. Her inside (right) leg is on to help with the bending, and her outside (left) hand is giving enough to allow him to bend.

2. Then she "throws away" the reins by pushing her hands and elbows forward, and Cohiba begins to stretch his head down and his nose out a little bit. Compare this "right" way with . . .

LESSON 14

Stretching Him
Long and Low

IF YOU SUCCESSFULLY COMPLETED our previous lesson, "Put Him on the Aids," your horse should now willingly come forward from your leg; step toward the bit; yield to your hand; give his jaw in a fluid, soft, elastic way; and feel equal in both reins and bend evenly in either direction—*most* of the time.

Why not all of the time? Because, as I told you, he'll probably be able to stay on the aids at the walk, trot, and canter long before he can handle transitions—those significant challenges to his balance (and yours)—without rooting or sticking his head in the air.

I also urged you not to fight your horse over this, because you could set up a resistance that would destroy everything else you'd worked for. Better to look the other way in the transition, maintain passive contact, let him do whatever he's going to do, and then reestablish a good rhythm and ask him to come round, soft, and supple again. Transitions, I said, were a lesson for another day.

Now We Get to Transitions

Well, that day is here. And transitions won't be just a lesson for this day; they'll be central to our focus over the next several lessons as we work on the all-important subject of keeping your horse on the aids through every possible combination of frame, stride, and tempo. Why? To improve suppleness and elasticity. Ultimately, to achieve the ability not only to shorten his stride while shortening his frame (most people can do that), but to shorten his stride while *lengthening* his frame, or even lengthen his stride while shortening his frame. Also to refine the basic control you've already created over the placement of his head, hindquarters, and middle until you can control the height of his neck and the flexion at his poll: neck low and long and flexed, neck low and long and nose out, head up and nose out, head up and nose in, head up and bent to the right, head down and bent to the left . . .

All in all, that's a tremendous reper-

3. . . . a very typical "wrong": Instead of pushing her hands forward, toward Cohiba's mouth, Erin's put them down. This may give her a sense of reaching, but it doesn't give her horse a loose rein. He's hit the bit and is starting to duck rather than stretch.

4. *Now* he's really getting the stretch idea—and to give him that total sense of freedom he may need, Erin's leaned forward and come a little bit out of the saddle. That's fine; she's getting the job done. Note that her hands are going straight toward Cohiba's mouth, not down toward his shoulders.

toire, a huge addition to your dressage vocabulary, and a gigantic increase in your horse's athleticism, comfort, and ridability.

Another "Non-Classical" Solution

We're going to start developing what I call your horse's "squishability" (his through-ness) by teaching him to stretch long and low smoothly and willingly, then smoothly come back up again. Of course, in an ideal world, if he's been working correctly on the aids, with power energetically coming from behind, when you ride him a little bit forward and put your arms a little forward to offer him the reins, he'll naturally seek your hand by reaching gently down toward the bit and stretching his nose toward the ground. But this is the *real* world—and if he's gone for any length of time with his nose poked out and his head in the air and the muscles of his back contracted and tense, if he hasn't always been worked correctly, if he's resistant or suspicious, or even if he's just a bit clueless, you'll need to use a few little tricks to "show him the way to the ground." Once the light dawns, he will quickly learn to love stretching in all its variety—with no contact, on contact, with you placing his neck at different heights, and finally down and flexed. (You may even find he likes stretching so much that he wants to snatch the reins from your hands when you offer—a "no-no" I'll tell you how to fix.)

In Lesson 15 we'll move on to keeping your horse on the aids during transitions within gaits—medium walk to free walk, say, or lengthened trot to working trot. From there we'll go on to asking him to stay on the aids during transitions between gaits, such as trot to walk or trot to canter. By the time we've wrapped up our focus on transitions, you'll be that

much closer to where I told you we were going in our very first lesson together: "Eventually you can ask him to do anything—go fast, go slow, put his head up, put his head down, straighten, go crooked, shorten his body, lengthen, piaffe, gallop down a hill, or make a quick rollback turn in the jumping field." That is still—no, more than ever—our goal.

Why Stretch Long and Low?

Any athlete can tell you the importance of stretching before and after you work. You already stretch certain of your horse's muscles when you walk and trot around during your warm-up. And you stretch others when you bend him left and right. But the only way to stretch the all-important muscles of his topline—from his poll, down the top of his neck, to the muscles you sit upon that go all the way from his withers to his croup and tail—is to get him to stretch his nose to the ground. Ultimately, if he's working nicely on the aids, when you gradually open your fingers and give both arms forward toward his mouth, he should follow the bit as far as you give to him, stay there for five or fifty strides, and then, when you close your legs and bring your arms back, melt right back up into the frame you originally had.

What does this stretching accomplish?

• It's a great way to get your horse listening and on the aids when he's head-high, hollow, distracted, or "looky." Rather than fighting him and saying, "Get your head down, get your head down"—exactly the no-win battle so many of us get suckered into—you can practically overdo things in the opposite direction, almost to the point of being too low and too deep (a combination of riding him down toward the ground and riding him on the aids). Then you can back off all your aids and "allow" him to almost automatically come up into the frame you're after without a fight.

• It's a way to increase communication and cooperation. Once a horse understands stretching on request, I can improve a movement by simply riding his neck a little low if he's getting tight, or asking for a tiny change of bend if he's pushing into his shoulder.

• It's a required movement in Training Level Tests 3 and 4 and First Level Tests 1, 2, and 3, where it confirms the correctness of your horse's training by showing that he's truly on the aids. It shows that he's supple, yielding, relaxed, and pushing forward, with a back that's really working to transmit the energy from his hind legs over his back and neck to his poll. There the energy reaches down into your hand, which then has a way of directly controlling his hind-leg power.

• It's a wonderful tool for relaxing your horse when new situations or difficult movements challenge him. For example, if my horse starts to tense, tire, or tighten his back during sitting trot, I move into posting trot and let him stretch down. (Any horse, but especially a green one, can take sitting trot for only so long.) Or, if he's having trouble with canter pirouettes, I put him on a large canter circle and reach my hands forward to encourage him to stretch his head to the ground; I let the stretch restore the jump, roundness, and elasticity of his canter. Then I sit back, close my leg, bring him back together, and return to a new and improved canter pirouette.

STRETCHING WITH CONTACT

1. When Erin keeps a feel of the mouth, Cohiba starts out tentatively, stretching his head and neck about as much as he did on a loose rein in photo 2 on page 86.

2. She perseveres, and here she gets almost the same withers-to-poll stretch as she had on a loose rein in photo 4 on page 87. Again, I have no problem with her leaning forward—Cohiba is so low that if she didn't, and if he suddenly brought his head up, she'd have to reel in a lot of rein.

(Continued on next page)

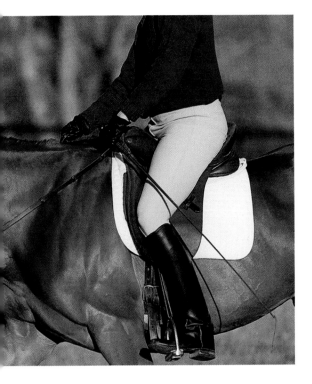

**STRETCHING WITH
CONTACT** *(continued)*

3. Another typical "wrong": Erin's bending hand is low and back on her thigh, pulling backward, which is making Cohiba duck his chin and "break" his neck behind the poll. What we're looking for is not the head down, but the neck down and the head out. She needs to try again, keeping her leg on to encourage him forward as she gives.

4. Before moving to the canter, we made sure Cohiba had a pretty good idea of what stretching is about. This— neck low, nose out—is a very good stretch for him, because he likes to duck. And he's not overflexing. You're seeing a very low neck and a face that seems slightly behind the vertical—but look at the angle of the head to the neck. Bring his neck up to a normal level, maintain the same angle of head to neck, and he's way in front of the vertical.

You'll Succeed If You . . .

• Tailor your stretching program to your horse. If he's very tight, uphill, and above the bit, ask him to stretch several times during each schooling session. If he has good balance and a nice elastic body, stretch him once or twice a few times a week. And if he's dramatically on the fore-hand, teach him how to stretch, check now and again to make sure he remembers, but otherwise stay away from stretching until his balance improves.

• Have a friend watch you. Believe me, when your horse stretches straight down from the withers and puts the tip of his nose at knee level, you're going to feel as if his front end has disappeared and he's about to tip over. And if he only stretches to elbow level, you may believe—almost everybody does, when feel is all they have

to go on—that he's stretching farther than he is. Either way, a friend's eye gives you a good reality check.

• Make sure your horse doesn't fake you out by breaking in the middle of his neck, rather than dropping from the base of his neck in front of the withers. If he *is* fak-ing, you'll see a bump in his neck, rather than an even curve from withers to poll (see photo 3 below)—so you'll know he's ducking "behind the bit" rather than honestly stretch-ing toward it. No quick fix here, but don't panic; just continue persistently with the exercise I describe below to get him to give you an honest stretch. However . . .

• STOP if it ain't working. If you don't get results after a few days, continued fuss-ing will just drive both of you nuts. Find someone who can give you good, solid, professional guidance.

Teach Him to Stretch

Walk your horse on a big circle to his more difficult (OK, stiffer) direction—let's say it's the right—because stiffness on the inside is always easier to "break up." Use your legs to support and maintain the walk, and to keep him from slowing or stopping, but not to push him anywhere. Now bend him very quickly to the right—he knows how to do that—and as soon as he softens and gives, throw both reins away, almost as if to prevent the weight of them from pulling his head down. You may have to start with reins we'd normally consider too long (not an entirely elegant picture), and you may have to lean forward or put your chest on his neck to give him enough room, but I want *no* contact, *no* connection, and *no* fudging. The three biggest problems I encounter teaching this

"trick" are that riders start with their reins too short, that they don't give the reins quickly enough, and that they don't make the reins truly, sloppily loose. And I guarantee: Horses have a sixth sense that tells them when you're not giving them the room to go all the way down without running into the bit.

If your horse does reach down, he may go only 2 or 3 hesitant inches. He may reach down so far (to the point where his nose is at the level of his knees is ideal) that, as I mentioned before, you feel as if he's going to tip over or fall on his front end. You may have a very scary, insecure sensation because there's "nothing" in front of you. He may speed up or slow down.

That's OK! If he offers *anything* in a downward direction, don't be afraid to LET GO (even if he does hurry or wander off the circle), pat him, praise him, tell him what a good guy he is—and then make any adjustment that's necessary.

And if he doesn't reach down? Gather the reins back up and try bending him very much right, then very much left, then very much right, then throwing the reins away and really *solidly* patting him on the top and sides of his neck to make him aware of the muscles you want him to stretch.

After you've gained the control to be able to get your horse to stretch for several strides whenever you ask—which could take ten minutes or ten days—use all your tact and sensitivity to carefully shorten the reins and reestablish contact, carefully establish a little inside bend, carefully ask him to flex and come on the aids, and then carefully bring him back up to the level you want by inviting rather than forcing him. Once he has the idea of stretching without contact, start pushing your arms forward and maintaining light contact, so you encourage him to follow the bit down to the ground.

At this point, your horse may start snatching the reins, as if to say "I remember this and I like it." Overlook the snatching for a day or so. (I'll do *anything* to give a horse the feel of stretching down!) Then close your fingers and lock your arms as you offer the reins. By jerking himself, he'll start learning that this exercise is about communication and suppleness, and that he can only stretch down as much and as rapidly as you ask him to do. ∎

SHORTENING THE WALK

1. As Courtney begins to shorten this nice normal walk, Ghirahdelli (an eight-year-old warmblood) does his thing: coming a little above and against the bit and shortening his neck. To keep him on her aids, she's sliding the bit on his tongue, making it "alive" and more difficult to pull against: moving the right rein—NOT pulling back—by just closing her fingers or moving her arm a tiny amount, then softening that rein and moving the other one. She's shifted her weight back a little (see "Using Your Back" on page 96) but has collapsed slightly; we want her to keep her chest up and forward. Her leg is back correctly to keep him from slowing too much.

2. In compressing his stride (compare his hind legs here and in photo 1), Ghirahdelli's also compressed his whole body, shortening his neck. Keeping the bit alive on his tongue—here Courtney's moving her left rein, so the right bit ring is against his face—has kept him on the aids; he's accepting them well. She's lifted her chest (though her knee and heel could be down more) and stopped following his movement with her back.

LENDON'S CHALLENGE

Can you shorten the walk without having your horse tighten or brace anywhere in his body?

On the Aids:
Transitions Within Gaits

ALTHOUGH WE STARTED PUTTING your horse "on the aids" two lessons ago, up until now we haven't worried about *keeping* him on the aids in transitions. (One thing at a time is my motto.)

In this lesson, though, we're going to use transitions within gaits to . . .

- further increase communication
- develop more control over frame, stride, and tempo
- improve the coordination of your weight, hand, and leg aids—the half-goes and half-halt ideas that ultimately, over time, will become true, classical, working half-halts
- and test and improve your horse's throughness or squishability. If he can't adjust frame, stride, and speed while staying responsive, light, and elastic, stepping forward, and yielding his jaw and poll—if the transition disrupts him in any way, be it by making him throw his head in the air or making him hit the bit and get hard in your hand—he isn't through.

We'll go from a medium walk, working trot, and working canter to a bigger, more forward walk, trot, and canter, and from medium walk and working trot to a shorter walk and trot. (A slower, shorter canter is probably still more than your horse is ready for.) In our next lesson, we'll move on to transitions between gaits with trot/walk/trot. In Lesson 17, we'll put your riderless horse back on the longe to introduce trot/canter/trot. And in Lesson 18, we'll put you back in the saddle for trot/canter/trot transitions on and off the longe.

Your eventual goal—anywhere, anytime; be it in a slow walk, extended canter, piaffe, or pirouette—is to do no more than "breathe on your horse's side with your leg," barely move your fingers on the rein, and immediately feel him lengthen or come together. The bad news: Such an ultimate state of squishability may take years to achieve. The good news: You should see at least *some* response and improvement within a month. So (I hate to beat you over the head with this, but . . .) if, after a couple of months, your horse remains obstinately clueless and uncooperative, either not going forward from your leg or insistently boring down or throwing his head in the air in response to your hand, it just ain't workin'. Stop doin' it on your own and get some qualified professional help.

Three Keys to Success

- Know your horse. If he's like most horses (and you're like most riders), shortening and lengthening will be easiest at the walk, and the walk will be easiest to return to if things fall apart at the trot or canter. But if he's one of those few horses that do not work well in the walk (for example, horses that have had a lot of not-so-great Western training tend to jig nervously, get fussy, or refuse to touch the bit), help him by starting with the natural momentum of the trot.

FORWARD AND BACK IN THE TROT

1. Forward with bending: If your horse puts his head in the air in transitions, bending him this much just before (even during) the transition will encourage him to stay elastic; he won't be able to brace straight against both reins. As he improves, reduce the amount of bend. Courtney's right rein, back and slightly open, is asking for the bend; her left (outside) arm is following to allow the bend. Too many riders either drop the contact altogether or take on the inside rein but don't follow with the outside rein. Her inside leg is nicely on the girth, but her outside needs to be back more in case Ghirahdelli tries to throw his haunches out.

2. Ghirahdelli's pushing well from behind in a nice long stride, but he's getting on his forehand—a common problem when a green horse is asked to maintain longer strides before he's ready. Going forward for just a few strides and then coming back helps teach him to shift his weight rearward and keep his balance. Courtney's bending him a little to prepare to . . .

• Stay elastic in your mind and body. Patience is a virtue, but I actually see more problems resulting from rider rigidity than from hurrying. Your horse can never be more elastic and supple than you are. If he gets a little strong and resistant, don't grab the reins and hang. For every rider who succeeds by doing that, there are hundreds who just can't win, because horses are a whole lot stronger than people. The only sure way to get positive results is to be smarter than your horse and use the many and varied tools I give you.

• Add shortening and lengthening to your everyday work—it's something I do every day with every horse. Even when my Grand Prix partner Last Scene was seventeen and I'd been riding him for a dozen years, after I'd gotten on and we'd waddled around a bit, I'd still pick up the reins and ask him to come a little deep, to shorten, to lengthen. That stuff is all about "on the aids." It's suppleness and elasticity. It's throughness. It's a way of life—and the way any horse should be.

And what does it become? Half-halts: those things we use nonstop. Believe me, I'm out there making little adjustments to stride—a little go, a little whoa—all the time. And I'll tell you something else. When I ask for the responsiveness and adjustability and they aren't there, even if I'm riding a Grand Prix horse, I change whatever plans I had for the day's work. I say, "Today we don't even *think* about piaffe, passage, flying changes, half-pass. Today we go back and

LENDON'S CHALLENGE

When you bend your horse to keep him on the aids as he lengthens, do his poll and nose stay at the same height?

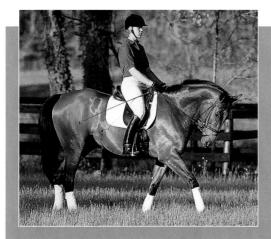

WRONG: Instead of bending, Ghirahdelli's evaded the aids by ducking his chin toward his chest—though to Courtney he may feel as if he is bending. In a true bend (see photo 1 below), your horse stretches and makes the outside of his neck longer while keeping his poll at the same height; you feel him pushing forward the same amount from behind. To prevent this evasion, make sure that (1) your inside leg keeps asking him to come forward and gives him that little bit of "post" around which he can bend, (2) your outside arm allows him to bend, and (3) you're not hanging on the reins as you bend—if you do, he'll collapse from the pressure. Ask for the bend, get it, and then soften. (If ducking is a habit, try lifting your inside hand to lift his head as you give him a little kick to remind him to come forward.)

3. . . . shorten his stride. Now we see a very different picture. He's shifted his weight back, carrying more on that left hind leg, so his front has come up a little. Courtney's behind her leg (which is turning out), sitting on the back of the saddle. Why? In photo 2, she had too much weight against her knee roll and not enough down through her lower leg and heel. When she sat taller (taller, NOT back!) to help bring her horse back, her leg went farther forward and her seat came back to compensate. But even though she's out of balance, she hasn't grabbed his mouth. Her hands are even, her feel is soft—and he's stayed on the aids.

USING YOUR BACK

Lifting your chest makes you sit a little deeper—stronger—into the saddle. That pressure closes the door on your horse's hind end and reinforces anything else you're saying to him. If you increase your leg, your stronger seat will help activate his hind legs in a collected way. If you use more hand, your seat will help get the hind end to shorten and so slow or stop him.

Your long-term goal is to use as little hand as possible. With regular practice, your horse will associate the change in your weight and your still back with your closing fingers and your voice aid, so he'll learn to come back from just your weight shift.

1. Her shoulder and hip aligned, Courtney is following the motion of the stride with her "normal" back.

2. To slow the stride, she stops following the motion and lifts her chest ("thrusts the bust") a little more, bringing her upper body back just a tad. Her alignment hasn't changed, and she's NOT leaning behind the vertical.

restore the quality and squishability of our walk, trot, and canter."

Shorten and Lengthen at the Walk

Pick up a normal (medium) walk on a loose rein. Take up a passive contact without having anything change. Then ask your horse to come on the aids by closing your leg and pushing him a little bit more forward. Lift your chest (or, as I like to put it, "thrust the bust"), which makes you sit a little taller and deeper in the saddle, and briefly close your fingers more firmly on the reins, encouraging him to give his jaw and come round, so the stepping-forward energy you generate surges up from his hind legs through his back, over his poll,

and down to his mouth. There you can control it right back to your hands.

That's the ideal. If you've got that, you've got a lot. If you don't, remember the ways I gave you to help your horse along. If he doesn't step forward from your leg, give him a little whack with the stick. If he pops his head up or hits against your hand, make sure you haven't stiffened your arms or body; then bend him to the inside, slide the bit on his tongue, or take-and-give on the inside or outside rein. Experiment; see what works for him.

Now ask your horse to shorten stride: Lift your chest to shift your weight back (but don't lean) and, keeping your leg against him, close your fingers on the reins—not to stop him or kill the walk, but

to walk him up into a slightly shorter, rounder frame.

Will it work just like that? Not always. This may be one of those aids you'll have to educate your horse to respond to by finding the right coordination of aids and teaching him this is something he can do. So if he throws his head or hits against the bit, first make sure you're not pulling too hard on his mouth. Then return to your medium walk (I call it your "neutral zone") and put him back on the aids by coordinating just the right amount of leg and hand and using one of the same little tools that helped you to get him round in the first place—a little bending, a little sliding of the bit, a little take-and-give. Keeping him a little bent, ask him to shorten again; as soon as he responds, squeeze with your leg, push your hands forward, and immediately return to a medium walk. With all these transitions, your goal is not to have him trundle along slowly but to have him stay on the aids while he shortens and goes forward again.

Next, ask your horse to lengthen his stride: Close your legs alternately (right leg when his right hind is about to step forward, left leg when his left hind is about to step forward), and put your arms forward just enough to let his neck get a bit longer and his frame stretch. If you feel his shoulders reaching more forward and his hind legs stepping farther under, chances are he's "through." If you don't feel that, or if he leans on the bit, he may have lost balance—or you may have dropped the reins and lost the connection. Return to the medium walk, restore the basic qualities and coordination of "on the aids," and then repeat the transition with more tact, subtlety, and, if necessary, cleverness—using one of your tools: bending, sliding the bit, or take-and-give on one rein.

Shorten and Lengthen at the Trot; Lengthen at the Canter

Let me make five things perfectly clear.
1. We are not talking about the outer limits of collection and extension. We're talking about a teeny bit smaller and a teeny bit bigger.
2. You're welcome to post the trot, but don't overlook the slower trot as a nice opportunity to practice sitting.
3. The gaits may differ from the walk, but the theory stays the same. You're simply looking for your horse to stay light, elastic, and willing to go forward from your leg and come back from your hand.
4. Make sure your horse can stay consistently on the aids through the shorter, medium, and longer walk and trot before you try lengthening stride at the canter.
5. Slowing the trot and canter is a wonderful test of your ability to find the balance point—just enough leg that your horse doesn't slam on the brakes and drop to a lower gait, and just enough hand that you're not hanging on him or making him dive down.

Again, I'm going to hit you over the head with "If you try it ten times and it doesn't work, come up with a different way of doing it." If your horse keeps throwing his head when you ask him to go forward, for example, put him on a circle and bend him to the inside as you ask with your leg. He'll have much more trouble sticking his head up when he's bent. And if, when you ask him to come back, he hits your hand, put him on a circle and bend him or slide the bit on his tongue. ■

> "If you try it ten times and it doesn't work, come up with a different way of doing it."

1

2

LENDON'S CAVEAT

Leg-yield through the transition only as a *short-term corrective exercise*. Yes, it almost magically helps you keep your horse round and not bracing. But overdo it and you'll teach him to pop his shoulder—which could be just about as big a problem.

LESSON 16

Transitions Between Gaits:
Trot/Walk/Trot

3

FIX A TROT/WALK TRANSITION BY LEG-YIELDING

My educated guess tells me that Toddingham, an eight-year-old Cleveland Bay, will brace in this downward transition—so I'll beat her to the punch with a leg-yield to break up tightness in her back, counter her inclination to fall on her inside shoulder, and keep her from sticking her head in the air. The tricky part? Using aids that ask for two distinctly different responses—a transition from trot to walk and a leg-yield—may confuse her. I'll keep things as clear and uncomplicated as possible by using an aid you can't see—my voice—to ask for the walk itself.

Let's see how it works on a trot circle:

1. I stop posting, stretch up, sit a little heavier, and say, "WA-aaalk," as I take a little extra bend to the right and close my leg to encourage Toddingham to step to the left. She responds by staying round, crossing her right hind leg a little bit, and . . .

2. . . . coming to the walk with a definite "side-wayness," roundness, and crossing of her right fore. If you think the bend has increased, you're right. It's not because I'm pulling on the right rein, though, but because my left leg is fairly passively allowing my right leg to push her left shoulder out. Within another step . . .

3. . . . she's a very soft horse, crossing over easily and keeping her left shoulder underneath her because my left leg is saying, "Good girl! You stayed round and bent in the transition. Now let's walk forward and straight on the circle."

THE DAY IS COMING WHEN YOU'LL be able to ask your horse to do anything at a moment's notice—go fast, go slow, lift or lower his head, straighten or get crooked, shorten or lengthen, gallop down a hill, make a quick rollback turn in the jumping field—and have him immediately and athletically respond.

In Lesson 15, we used transitions within gaits—medium walk to lengthened walk, for example—to increase communication; refine the coordination of your weight, hand, and leg aids; and test your horse's throughness or squishability. (When he's through, he can adjust his frame, stride, and speed without throwing his head in the air, hitting the bit, getting hard in your hand, or falling on his forehand.) Now we're going to add those major challenges to his and your balance and coordination: transitions between gaits.

Why are transitions between gaits SO difficult? Because you've got about one second and one step to do the transition (change from a four-beat walk to a two-beat trot, for example), put it all together, and get it right.

When you're working on getting your horse on the aids, you can go around and around for ten minutes figuring it out. But a transition is a momentary thing; you can't say, "I think I'm getting it . . . I'm getting it . . . I've almost got it . . . OK, I've got it." No matter how gradual you try to make a transition, it still comes down to that one instant when he switches from one gait to the other.

So I'll try to make transitions more doable by breaking them down

into bite-sized pieces, with plenty of trouble-shooting included. In this lesson we'll delve into trot/walk/trot. (Walk/halt/walk is actually simpler—but not for a young and/or green horse who may have difficulty standing still on the bit.)

Ready? Hold up, my friend. First, let me ask you a question about your riding.

Which Came First . . .

. . . the chicken or the egg? Do you lose your balance because your horse lurches from the walk into the trot (or from the trot into the walk)? Or does he lurch into the trot because your leg isn't underneath you, keeping you balanced so you can help him make a good transition?

That is the question to answer before you're in the middle of transitions, and now is as good a time as any (probably better than most) to reevaluate your balance, relaxation, and independence of aids. Why? Because no matter what happens—whether your horse lurches, drags, throws his head up, pokes his

1. I check out Toddingham's bendability by bending her right on the trot circle for two or three strides, then left two or three strides, then right, then left again. Then I ask for the walk through the bend: I keep my right leg at the girth (my left is a little behind the girth) and gently bend her right as I stop posting, stretch up, sit a little heavier, and say, "WA-aaalk."

2. A neat moment: My right leg is now back (my left is at the girth) and I'm ever-so-softly bending her to the left by *allowing with* (not dropping) the right rein. She, in turn, is staying round and taking a slightly shorter, less energetic trot step that tells me the next step will be . . .

3. . . . . the first step of walk. Once again, my right leg is at the girth and my left hand is a little bit forward, allowing the right bend *and* maintaining contact.

4. A stride or two later, I'm bending her to the left one more time, and she's completing a round, on-the-aids transition by walking energetically forward.

LENDON'S CAVEAT

This is a fix, a correction, a "busy-ness" for preventing or overcoming a bad habit on your horse's part (or a tightening or locking up on your part). Sliding the bit and bending left and right must not—I repeat, MUST NOT—become a way of life.

READY TO LONGE
(continued)

stirrups so they won't bounce. And—an especially important canter-work precaution—I've tightened the girth securely; the last thing I want is his saddle sliding around! I've attached the side reins to the billets at about the bottom of the saddle flaps, so they'll be pretty much parallel to the ground when he's in a correct frame, with his poll the highest point and his face on or a tiny bit in front of the vertical. Now about that frame: Through a slow, deliberate process—adjusting two holes at a time, watching, stopping, adjusting again—I've gradually tightened the side reins to where I can achieve the goal of this exercise: showing Idocus that he can go from trot to canter without throwing his head in the air or coming above the bit. Actually, he's neither green nor tough on this issue—if he has any tendency, it's to drop a little behind. But if he were a flipper or a puller, the shorter side-rein length that's normally correct for the canter could position him almost uncomfortably behind the vertical at the halt, the walk, even the trot.

you're both comfortable: with him on the longe. (If the two of you worked through Lesson 8, our walk/trot longe lesson, he understands the idea and the equipment, and you understand the technique.) By not only removing any shred of rider interference but also stabilizing him with side reins, longeing lets you teach him that he can find his balance and canter without flinging his head, and that he can come back to trot without running or going splat on his forehand.

Longeing will give you one other advantage as well. It'll let you see what you must do under saddle to help your horse make the transition smoothly and maintain that balance, because . . .

Timing Is Everything

We all know that the canter is a three-beat gait, but did *you* know that your horse takes the first step of his canter stride exactly where you'd least expect—on the outside hind? You can maximize his chances of picking up the correct lead without resistance, hops, or juggle steps if you ask when he's most ready: at the moment his outside hind is coming forward and preparing to push off!

Can't feel that happening? Longeing allows you to *see and study it*. Not that I want you to get hung up on timing! Just be aware of it, because it's something we will eventually add to your riding repertoire.

Cantering on the Longe Can Be Dangerous . . .

. . . if your horse panics, bolts, races, bucks, rears, kicks out, plays, or drags you off your feet. Although I don't want you to expect the worst, I do want you to do everything possible to anticipate and prevent it, so . . .

• Longe on good footing.
• Work in a corner, where the two sides can help you guide, control, and (as I'll explain in a moment) emergency-stop your horse.

• Use a cotton-web longe line (so you can hang on securely), 10 to 12 meters long (that's 30 to 35 feet) so you can work him on a comfortably large circle.
• Wear gloves; ribbon the longe line over your palm (NEVER wrap it around your hand); and stand with shoulders back, elbows bent, arms at your side, knees bent, and the foot closer to your horse's haunches a half-step behind the foot closer to his head, so you can either give-and-take or lean back and brace.
• Always—and I mean ALWAYS—stay out of range of your horse's hind feet. If you don't, and he kicks into the circle, even in play, you could get your face bashed in.

To Make Cantering on the Longe Productive . . .

• Spend the first week—about six sessions—starting on your horse's stronger or suppler side. After that, start every other session on his weaker or stiffer side.
• Canter a few strides—half a circle at first—so your horse doesn't break to the trot. Tell him to trot before he breaks and he'll gradually learn to canter longer and wait for you.
• Longe for no more than half an hour, change direction every five minutes—and, whenever possible, quit while you're ahead. For example, if you start disastrously in the first direction but then improve even a little bit, stop. Your horse won't get one-sided in one day, and you'll have made a point and had some success.
• Make sure your horse is promptly obedient to your aids. You can have all the timing in the world, but if he's a little dead or ho-hum about your aids, none of it is going to work. The canter aids mean "Canter *now*"—not "Oh, you said 'canter.' OK now, lemme see, I guess maybe I'll think about picking up the canter."

1. Here we have a horse going very freely and exuberantly forward. If he suddenly kicked out or took off, I could get hurt. So I'm standing well out of range of his hind legs. My whip is pointing down behind me (not toward his haunches, where it could egg him on). I've "ribboned" the extra longe line over the palm of my right hand. And I'm holding the line to the bit in my left hand exactly the way I'd hold a rein, my arm in the same bent-elbow-at-my-side position. I'm also standing with my left foot leading, my right foot back, and my knees a little bent: a reactive but solid position for anything exciting that might happen. (I'm standing very slightly ahead of Idocus's shoulder. He's trying to cut in and make the circle smaller, and I'm trying to encourage him to enlarge it.)

LENDON'S CHALLENGE

Can you keep your horse in the same round frame through the walk, trot, canter, and transitions by repeatedly adjusting and readjusting the side reins?

2. That's more like it! The longe line could be a bit tighter, but Idocus has settled into an active trot with a nice frame and a good stretch into the side reins. Now that he's pushing forward and softly reaching to the bit, with his back round, I can start to watch his diagonal pairs of trot legs and think about timing the canter transition. If I say "Can-TER" at the very moment his right hind starts coming forward, he can, in the next split second . . .

3. . . . . plant that foot firmly, thrust his body strongly forward . . .

TROT/CANTER TRANSITIONS ON A LOOSE REIN

These help me remove any reason for Toddingham to come above the bit and brace her back, body, or hind legs against the reins.

1. At the trot, I "break" any inclination the mare may have to brace: My strong inside leg at the girth serves as both a post around which I bend her and a pusher with which I move her over toward my supporting outside rein. My inside rein asks her to soften, round, flex, and bend (here a little too much) to the inside.

2. I maintain a centered body position (no toppling forward), immediately put both arms forward to soften on the

LENDON'S CHALLENGE

Can you give both your hands forward at the moment of the canter depart, so you neither restrict nor help your horse?

LESSON 18

Trot/Canter Transitions
Under Saddle

IN LESSON 17, WE ASKED YOUR horse to do trot/canter transitions on the longe, where you stabilized him with side reins and without any possibility of rider interference. Now—provided he's trot/cantering and canter/trotting calmly and responsively on the longe—we're going to go ahead and give 'em a try under saddle (I'll tell you how in a moment).

If your position is correct and your hands and legs are sufficiently clear and quiet so all goes smoothly and well, that's great! But if your horse stiffens and braces, if he doesn't respond because your aids are unclear or confusing, or if he flings his head because you're either throwing him away or catching him in the mouth, you're just not ready to go it alone. Get off, put him back

in his side reins, and longe him to loosen him up and to make sure the side reins are correctly adjusted and his transitions are still good. (For safety's sake, always undo the side reins when mounting and dismounting.) Then climb back on and ask your helper to longe him with you on his back while you figure things out through the "babiest" of baby steps:

1. Passive seat and hand— where your helper calls all the shots while you just hold a loose rein and exist

as simple weight on your horse's back—so you can explore exactly what happens with your body and his

2. Active seat and passive hand—where your helper is still supportive but you start asking for transitions with leg and seat

3. Active seat and active hand—where you put all your aids together and connect completely with your horse (but with the side reins and your helper still there to steady him).

Once you're comfortable, fluid, and consistent on the longe, go back out on your own, where, just as on the longe . . .

You'll Succeed If You . . .

• Turn off the tightness. You *must* relax in order to go with your horse. Whenever you feel yourself tightening (or your helper says you're stiffening or "clamping on"), stop! Change your focus and your state of mind—not by walking on a loose rein (which just makes my students stew about their tension), but by doing something totally different, such as a couple of minutes of the stretching, balancing, and loosening exercises I gave you in Lesson 9.

• Focus on the transitions. I don't mean trot/canter/trot/canter/trot/canter. I mean trot until it's good; then canter. And canter until it's good; then trot. And if you have to spend a lot of time fixing either the trot or the canter, you didn't listen when I said we can't do transitions until the basic gaits are good.

• Warm up until your posting trot

reins, and in the next split second ask for a right-lead canter, saying, "Go ahead and pick up the canter completely on your own. I'm not going to hang on you or hit you in the mouth, and I'm certainly not going to give you anything to brace against."

3. In the second beat of the canter stride, my arms are still forward, my reins are loose—and look at Toddingham! She's round, relaxed, and happily on the aids.

4. As we complete our first full canter stride with the downward phase (she's about to put all her weight on her inside lead leg), I return to a fairly normal connection between leg and hand. She stays soft and unbraced.

TROT/CANTER TRANSITIONS ON NORMAL CONTACT

Even in a regular trot/canter transition, I do everything I can to give Toddingham no reason to brace against me.

1. At the midpoint of the trot stride, I use a little inside bend to position her around my inside leg, bring her to attention—just a "Yoo-hoo, we're going to do something"—and test her throughness. If she doesn't respond, there's no way she's going to stay round in the canter depart. She bends nicely, though, so in the very next step . . .

2. . . . . I give my inside hand forward, "allow" her to come more straight, and . . .

3. . . . . in the next step, just as her outside hind is lifting, ask for the canter depart by smoothly sliding my left leg behind the girth. You can't see that, but you can see that I stay centered and square in the saddle, not leaning or shifting my hips from one side to the other. At this stage, getting hung up on weighting the seat bones or activating one more than the other will just make you crooked and your leg aids uneven. It won't

make you a more effective rider.

4. This and photos 5 and 6 show you three different scenarios as Toddingham pushes off her outside hind into the first "uphill" step of canter: Here I'm saying, "Canter, please, and I'll stay with you." My arms follow the motion; I maintain an even, nonrestrictive, teensy-bit-supportive feel of her mouth. Her body is straight, she's well framed between my legs and reins, and we have a very nice connection.

5. This is "Canter, please. Thank you." By throwing the inside rein away, I'm proving that Toddingham is yielding, through, and soft in my hand. I don't need that rein to hold her, any more than I'd need it to ride a circle.

6. But here she's gone against my hand and offered to raise her head—so I'm using the same inside leg and rein I used in the trot to tell her, "Canter, please, but stay with me, bend a little, don't throw that head up, and give to my rein aid."

(Continued on next page)

TROT/CANTER TRANSITIONS ON NORMAL CONTACT *(continued)*

7. Toddingham's in the second beat of the canter stride, on her inside-hind and outside-fore diagonal legs. Her body's mostly horizontal, her neck's a little lower, and my body's absolutely vertical. I've given my arms a little forward to stay with her and allow her to use her neck. (Look at the corner of her mouth: There's no more bit pressure than in photo 5, where the rein is loose.)

8. The final step of the canter stride, and the moment of truth for all riders—because

feels energetic and balanced—the best-quality trot you can get. Then do trot-walk and walk-trot transitions to make sure your goes and whoas are nicely in order and your horse is alert to your aids. Stretch him to the ground to get him thinking "head down," to see just how malleable he happens to be, and to check that you can bend him a little left and right. When you ask him to come back together, encourage him to keep a fairly low neck position—even a little *too* deep and extra-flexed as a reminder not to harden against you.

• Sit the trot to get the trot/canter transitions. You really *must* do this—because the very act of posting holds your horse in the trot. However, there's no point asking for the canter if your canter preparation is disruptive—so if you're so uncomfortable sitting that he hollows his back, slow and shorten the trot with a little half-halt idea. Then "sit" by getting as close to the saddle as you can while still sort of perching on your crotch.

• Do some detective work. If your horse does pretty nice trot-canter transitions when you're not on his back but either refuses or stiffens and braces when you are, he's telling you he remembers some kind of discomfort or associates pain with having a rider. If you feel yourself (or your helper sees you) clutching with your leg, falling back, thumping on his back, or irritating him with your aids, you need to do some work on your independence, balance, and security. And if you're actually riding quietly and well, persevere and let him know nothing's going to happen to disrupt or bother him. Things will improve.

The Trot/Canter Transition
After your warm-up on a large circle, slow the trot with a half-halt idea and sit: Lift your chest, so that your seat bones feel as though they're touching the saddle through your skin; keeping your legs closed, close your fingers and take back slightly to ask

your horse to shorten his trot for a stride. Then (see photo 1 on both page 110 and page 112) bend him an extra little bit to the inside—and the instant he gives, release the inside rein (soften; don't throw him away) and simultaneously tell him to canter: Sit squarely (don't worry about weighting this or that seat bone; just sit in the middle of him). Hold your inside leg at the girth and caress his side as you smoothly slide back your outside lower leg—without raising your heel—to a few inches behind the girth (just a slightly different position from "on the girth").

Ways not to give this leg aid (believe me, I've seen them all):

• Thinking you've slid your leg back when it hasn't moved at all

• Startling your happily trundling-along horse by taking your leg off and abruptly ("Ka-BLAM!") clamping it back on

• Raising your lower leg until it's almost horizontal and your heel is touching

or even lifting the bottom of your square saddle pad.

Give the aid correctly and your horse should canter within one or two strides—90 percent of all horses do. If yours doesn't, use your voice or a touch of the whip (liable to make him throw his head now but produce a better transition next time). When he does canter, press his side rhythmically with your inside leg to say "Let's keep it going" as you allow the more comfortable canter motion to settle you into the saddle.

Now, you're not exactly out of the woods yet. As I told you in Lesson 17, with the first step of canter your horse's weight rests on his outside hind and his body comes up in front; your body, which is "connected" to his back, comes a little forward and closer to his neck. In the second step, when he's on his diagonal inside hind/outside fore, his body is mostly horizontal; your body is pretty much vertical. But in the final step, all his weight is on his inside fore; his front end goes down, and your body goes slightly back.

The problem: Your arms, which are "connected" to his mouth, have to be relaxed, independent, and following to allow him to carry them forward. Otherwise you're going to interfere and jab him in the mouth! So sit almost vertically, keep your hips and lower back soft to absorb the back-and-forth motion, relax your shoulders—and whatever you do, don't freeze your elbows or clamp your armpits to your sides. You're not hatching eggs under there! Let those armpits air out and open those elbows a bit. I don't mean stick your elbows out. Just let a little air in and create a sense of your arms being able to go one way while your body goes the other.

This is simple, but it ain't easy. So give yourself time to practice. ∎

we have to be really honest with ourselves that we're giving the most we can. Toddingham is quite downhill, with almost all her weight on her leading right fore; I'm leaning back. Here the distance between my shoulder and her mouth is greater than at any other moment in the stride, so I really have to reach forward to keep the contact consistent. If I increased it by not following forward enough, she could open her mouth, tuck her chin in, or (what most horses do) take my hand as a fifth leg and balance on it.

9. We begin the next canter stride with all her weight once again on her outside hind. We're through the transition, the canter is getting established, my following arm is allowing her to move forward, and now we can get down to work. If I have one quibble, it's that I'm sitting a little in front of the vertical. But hey! If I'm going to err, it will always be in the direction of allowing her to go forward, freeing up her hind legs, and not jamming her back into the ground and making her sore!

LENDON'S CHALLENGE

Can you use weight and voice alone to go from canter to trot—so that in the transition and for a stride or two afterward, you can give your hand?

A NORMAL CANTER/TROT TRANSITION

For fun, let's take a little test: In photo 1, Toddingham is pushing off on her left hind leg and lifting her forehand. What gait is she in, which direction is she tracking, and where is she in the stride? If you answered, "Step one of the right-lead canter stride," good for you!

1. At a pleasant working canter, Toddingham's in a nice frame and slightly in front of the vertical. My lower leg is close and supportive, my seat is passive— and in this first step of the stride, when she's pretty uphill, my torso is slightly in front of the vertical and going "with" her. I've taken back a little on the right rein, possibly to bend her or ask her to soften and come no farther in front of the vertical. (Why my right hand is a touch lower than my left, I cannot tell you!)

Canter/Trot Transitions
Under Saddle

ONCE YOUR HORSE IS CANTER/ trotting calmly, smoothly, and responsively on the longe, go ahead and try this lesson's canter/trot transitions under saddle. (I'll tell you how in a moment.) If he stays relaxed, balanced, and obedient, you're doing just great! If, however, he doesn't, and you follow my suggestions for dealing with problems but he still stiffens, runs on, doesn't respond, or flings his head, go back to the longe and side reins and follow the same sequence of baby steps you took to figure out the trot/canter transition:

1. Passive seat and hand—you're a passenger holding a loose rein and simply exploring what happens to your body and your horse's.

2. Active seat and passive hand—your helper supplies the rein aids as you ask with leg and seat.

3. Active seat and active hand—you connect completely with your horse (but with your side reins and your helper still steadying him).

When you and your horse can do relaxed, fluid, consistent canter/trot transitions under saddle and on the longe, try them again on your own. And remember, just as in Lesson 18 . . .

You'll Succeed If You . . .

• Turn off the tightness. You must relax in order to go with your horse.

• Focus on the transitions. You're not earning mileage points, so trot until it's good, then canter; and canter until it's good, then trot.

• Warm up first. Post the trot to achieve energy and balance; use trot/walk and walk/trot transitions to make sure he's alert to your aids; stretch him to the ground and make sure he'll bend left and right to remind him not to harden against you and to get him thinking "head down."

In addition, I want you to . . .

• Make sure both of you are completely stabilized at the canter. He should be able to canter along nicely on his own without you

2. If you think of my body language as saying, "Hey, Toddingham, we're gonna whoa," this is "Hey, Toddingham, we're . . . " She is basically horizontal and centered on her diagonal legs; I'm changing from an "allowing" to a "telling" mode: lifting my chest, letting my "non-pinching" knee slide down to drop my heel a bit, and creating the sense of my seat bones going right down through my skin into the saddle (but not tucking my butt; despite what many people say, that's not "using your seat"). My torso is more on the vertical, my lower back has arched slightly, and my seat is much stronger in the saddle. I've even started asking something of her with my hands; she's giving her jaw, perhaps more than I'd like. Then again, my hands are higher than I'd like; I've lost the straight line from elbow to bit. In the very next step . . .

3. . . . . we're at the fleeting moment that begins the actual transition: the "whoa" part

A NORMAL CANTER/TROT TRANSITION *(continued)*

of my body language—and the third step of the canter stride, when you never want a picture taken because the moment looks so awkward. Toddingham's weight is on her inside fore (the right here), her hindquarters are in the air, and she looks very downhill. I've brought my upper body a little farther back and given forward with my arms, both to maintain a very definite contact and to avoid hitting her in the mouth. I'm also sitting down into the canter with the same quality of muscle relaxation as if I were sitting into her

holding on for dear life or whoaing or adjusting with every stride, which would just clutter his sensory perception and teach him not to hear your aids. So ask yourself: Can I let my aids subside? Can I follow with the softest contact? Can I leave him alone, see what I have, and adjust the canter to make it a little better balanced only when necessary?

When you can answer "yes" to all those questions, you're ready to try . . .

The Canter/Trot Transition

Your goal—and, yes, it may be long-term—is to ask for and get a smooth transition just by changing your weight, without doing anything with your hands. (In a moment I'll tell you what to do if this doesn't work, but first give it a good try!)

Establish a nice canter on a 20-meter circle. Then ask for the transition, using your body language to say "trot": Lift your head and chest (which automatically strengthens your lower back, allows your seat bones to come into the saddle, and

increases your security by sending more weight down through your legs), and stabilize your upper body—stop the slight forward-and-back rocking motion that kept you smoothly going with the canter. Using just your weight like this, see if your horse will trot nicely for you.

If he does, bravo! But if he continues to canter, say "trot" and give a short pull on his mouth, followed by a return to passive contact (repeat if necessary) to get the trot.

If your horse stays fairly soft in the transition, keep practicing—so that he gradually associates your weight change with the transition and needs less and less hand.

If you get the transition but he comes against or above the bit and/or develops a runny or on-the-forehand trot, he's still trying to figure out how to do a balanced downward transition. Next time, just before the transition, ask him to come a little "extra-through"—a little too deep—by bending him or sliding the bit. Then, in the motion of the transition, soften your hands so your aids are saying "Come on, keep

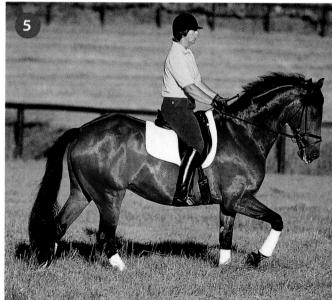

your body nice and soft (the bending or sliding), and now"—as you give—"come to trot."

If your horse *still* comes against or above your hand, continue bending or sliding the bit during the transition itself. Work with this subtly; as he improves, gradually reduce the bending and sliding. You may never be able to get a nice transition without some hand, but always have "minimal hand" as your goal.

Two ways NOT to ask for the canter/trot transition:
1. By leaning back behind the vertical and hauling on your horse's mouth
2. By tightening your buttock muscles. That's as big a no-no as you can commit, because it squeezes you up out of the saddle—which is exactly the wrong way to go.

Shared Responsibility

Of course, asking the wrong way isn't the only mistake you might make. Say your horse develops a runny or on-the-forehand trot; or say he shortens his stride, flings his

head in the air, tightens his back, and—bam . . . bam . . . bam—jounces you out of the saddle. He might (in a perfect example of the "chicken and egg" dilemma) be defending himself against your or a former rider's habit of grabbing and hanging—which you or she probably developed because he bounced you or her so much in the past.

If staying balanced is still a problem for *you*, the sliding-the-bit and bending corrections you used to correct stiffness, leaning, or head-flinging in trot-walk transitions may be more than you can pull off in the more rapid-fire canter-trot transitions. For now, until you're reliably able to go with your horse's motion, and even if he's on the forehand and scurrying, give him the first couple of strides: "Allow" your hands forward, and immediately post. And please, my friend, don't pick this moment to be heroic and sit the trot: Unless sitting the trot is super-easy for you, you'll just hang on his mouth and grab with your calves, heels, and hands—which will only encourage him to stiffen, run, or charge off even more.

After the first two strides, either . . .
• ask him promptly to walk (with continuing transitions, he'll begin to balance himself in anticipation of the requisite backward shift of his weight)
• set him back hard with a strong pull, followed by an immediate release (if you keep pulling, he has every right to pull back)
• or soften and supple him by sliding the bit or bending him.

If you continue to have difficulties, put the two of you back on the longe and spend more time building suppleness and improving your aids.

walk: my thighs and buttocks relaxed, my leg part of her side. In the next moment . . .

4. . . . her hind legs come through, the left hind "speeding up" to get in diagonal sync with the right fore as the right fore "slows down" and stays on the ground long enough to let the left hind catch up. In response, I'm giving my arm forward (notice the slightly more forward position of her nose), tucking my seat, and rounding my back to pick up the first bounce of the trot stride.

5. My back is straighter than in photo 4, but my forward arms and "going-with" upper body are still allowing Toddingham to trot forward and complete the transition.

6. With the first clean stride of trot, the mare's a little more on the aids, confidently coming forward into my hand, and nicely put back together again—because I didn't conk her in the mouth or bounce on her back in the transition.

For what to do when you've got a lot more horse to bring back, please turn the page.

A BIG CANTER/TROT TRANSITION

1. Here I have to steady Toddingham as she reshuffles her legs from canter to trot, even as I "allow" her—because she's got thrust coming out of her ears. My hands are forward, with a nice straight line between elbow and bit, but I close my lower leg and brace my back a bit.

2. Wow! The first step of trot, and she's both beautifully on the aids and not restricted in any way. Look at the bend of the joints in her right hind and left fore: She's very supple and POWERING forward. How do I sit the bounce phase of a trot like this? By softening my lower back to go with her.

3. Having allowed her to come forward with everything she's got, I can now—even as I follow her back throwing me into the air—brace *my* back, close my leg, and ask her to shorten stride, collect, and come back to me. She responds by coming up in her neck, staying nicely on the vertical, and stepping through on her left hind with a little more carrying power and a little less thrust. (Were there one more picture, you'd see me allowing again—because this kind of whoaing back is strictly a one-stride correction!) ∎

LESSON 20

Circles, Not Eggs!

IF YOU'VE BEEN STICKING WITH MY program, you should now be able to do any of the transitions between gaits called for in a Training Level test: trot/halt/trot, walk/trot/walk, or trot/canter/trot. In fact, if you can do a trot/canter transition and keep your horse on the aids, you're way ahead of many of the people competing at First Level!

But riding a dressage test isn't just a matter of a few transitions—especially not the way we school them at home, where Rule Number One is "only when everything's ready." A dressage test is a whole different ballgame, requiring you to . . .

- smoothly string together a series of movements without fading or falling apart
- ride accurate and correct figures—circles, serpentines, diagonals, even center lines (and let me tell you, I've ridden a lot of dressage tests that I could have won if it hadn't been for that center line)
- make transitions at the letters
- and read your horse from moment to moment.

Say the test calls for a left-lead canter transition at A. How does your horse feel approaching A? Is he more awake than usual? More lazy? Or is he unlike anything you've ever felt? (A horse show can do that, you know.) If he's in his "I'm ready" mode, you may not need your usual three strides to get the transition. If he's in his "Say what?" mode, you may need six. And if you've never before experienced the mode he's in, you're about to learn some-

thing really new about your horse and your riding.

So, to jump-start your and his competitive career, we're going to do . . .

A Test-Riding Miniseries

In this lesson we'll wean you off the vaguely "large" circles we used at home and teach you how to ride accurate 20-meter circles. We'll talk . . .

- the geometry of the circle, the difference between circles and corners, and the dressage arena they have to fit into (as well as how to build a simple arena if you don't have one)
- following the track by planning and using a "leading" eye

A 20-METER CIRCLE AT C

1. About a meter before C, Six Pack To Go and I are in a nice working trot. He's already got a little left bend, from his preparing for the turn onto the circle and continuing his bend coming out of the corner. I'm maintaining the bend by keeping my inside (left) leg closed at the girth, my inside hand back and slightly toward my outside hip, and my outside hand slightly forward and "allowing." I just wish somebody'd told me to straighten my outside wrist!

2. At C (next page), my focus is on where we're going—the point on the rail just beyond H—as I encourage Six Pack to start the circle by increasing his left bend. My inside leg at the girth helps create the impression that he's curving through his whole body, my outside leg is a bit behind the girth, and I've brought my outside hand a touch to the left (without crossing the

A 20-METER CIRCLE AT C *(continued)*

withers) to lay the outside rein firmly against his neck. My "leading" hand has also come left enough that the inside rein is off his neck. The result? Six Pack is "straight" on the circle, inside hind foot moving right into the print of inside fore. He is, however, showing a problem common to stiff horses and/or riders who hang on the outside rein: His inside ear is lower than his outside ear, his face is no longer on the vertical, and there's a bit of a twist in his neck.

3. Oops! His face is more on the vertical, but now he's *too* bent, as if his nose were on an 8-meter circle instead of the 20-meter one where his shoulders and hips are.

4. Almost a quarter of the way around the circle (we're about to hit the track just past H), his face is on the vertical, his ears are level, and he's "straight on the circle": His hind feet are stepping in the prints of his forefeet. My inside leg is at the girth, my outside leg slightly behind the girth; even though my outside rein is close to his neck to help bring him

LENDON'S CHALLENGE

Does your horse's bend match the curve of the 20-meter circle?

- the sequence and feel of your circling aids

- and avoiding or fixing common circle problems: too small, egg-shaped, inaccurate placement, inconsistent tempo, no bend, and collapsing over your inside leg. In the next few lessons, we'll talk about straight lines on the long side, diagonals, that darned center line, halts . . . and then we'll string movements together into a test.

Ready? Let's get showing!

Lendon's Little Geometry Lesson

A circle is a closed curved line, all points on which are equidistant from a center point. A large dressage arena is three times as long as it is wide: 20 by 60 meters. A small arena is two times as long as it is wide: 20 by 40 meters. Three 20-meter circles fit side-by-side in a large arena; two fit in a small arena. In a large arena, a perfect 20-meter circle touches the track at C, say, touches the track 10 meters from the corner on the next long side (not at the letter, which is only 6 meters from the corner), crosses the center line 20 meters from C, touches the next long side 10 meters from the corner, then returns to C. That same circle fits even more easily into a small arena, crossing the center line at X so you're looking straight ahead at E or B.

You'll want to show a demonstrable difference between corners (where you stay on the track and ride deeper in the corner) and circles (where you ride a continuous curved line that cuts the corner). The higher the level, the deeper the corner. The slower the gait, the deeper the corner. At the walk, even a Training Level horse should go fairly deep.

The bad news? You must ride in a dressage arena if you're to get comfortable riding 20-meter circles and corners. The

good news? Even if all you have is a big field, you can measure 66 feet (20 meters) and use ground poles, cones, paint buckets, even flowerpots to make yourself a ring—or the end of a ring—and mark the spots you have to hit.

You'll Succeed If You . . .

- Learn to react to *your* horse. I can give you general aids, but not exact aids that change from moment to moment. For example, your horse may need more inside

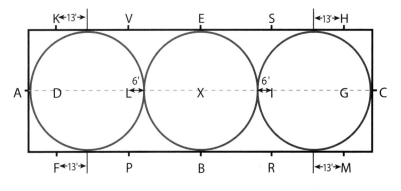

leg than I suggest for the bend you want. He may need more outside leg to keep from falling in because his haunches tend to swing out. And when his shoulder falls out, he may need a bit more outside rein against his neck. You may even find you need lots of inside leg as you start a circle, a little more outside rein once you get going, and more inside rein as you finish up. Finally, a circle to the left may feel completely different from one to the right and require totally different aids. You have to recognize that.

- Remember that the corrections I gave you for stiffness, leaning, or head-flinging during transitions will work on a circle, too. Any time your horse starts to push against the bit, get hollow, stiffen his back, or raise his head, take a small amount of extra bend or slide the bit a little.

- Dig out videos of the World

around, I'm still "allowing" the bend, the softness of the bit and the texture of the rein showing that I'm not restricting him in any way. Because I'm confident we'll meet the rail where we're supposed to, I've already shifted my focus to our next point on the center line.

Yes, circles are in meters, but it may help your accuracy to think of touching the track 13 feet from F and K and H and M—and of crossing the center line 6 feet from L and I.

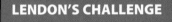

LENDON'S CHALLENGE

Can you ride a continuous curve, from short side to diagonal (and vice versa), that's deep enough into the corner to have a full stride on the track before M and after K?

CORNER TO CORNER

1. On the short side, approaching the corner, I'm looking a little past M onto the diagonal. I've established the bend I need for the corner: My right leg is obviously on (as my coming-up-badly heel shows!) to push Tucker into my connected outside rein and keep him from falling in. My outside rein is allowing and controlling the amount of bend. His hind feet haven't swung out, so my outside leg must be back. And I'm obviously sitting "into" him a little with my weight.

2. As we start the corner, I'm looking at the point where I'm going to leave the track, using as much of my bending aids as necessary to keep the flow. Without throwing the outside rein away, my feel there is allowing the bend. I'm using my right rein, but the bit is not pulled through Tucker's mouth, so you know

LESSON 21

Straight Lines:
Tracks and Diagonals

IN THIS LESSON WE'LL CONTINUE your dressage-show preparation with straight lines on the diagonal and on the track (both the long and the often-"fudged" short sides). I'll also explain how, why, and when to use your corners and turns to connect those straight lines properly (and not mess them up).

Let's start by talking straight lines.

From the Judge's Point of View

Your Training Level horse is understandably green—he's young or new to dressage, and you're just starting out in the sport. So it's less important that he be absolutely straight, with every vertebra from nose to tail in

perfect alignment, than that he appear *basically* straight: bending evenly in both directions throughout the test and not wildly throwing his haunches or leaning on one shoulder.

How do you create such an appearance? By consistently "positioning" him on the track in a teeny-tiny, itsy-bitsy inside *bend*—so he'll be prepared at a moment's notice to turn, circle, or ride a corner.

This positioning is a "technical" curve around your inside leg, so slight that it's almost more a feeling than an actual bend. Create it with your inside leg on the girth, "connected" to your outside rein. As you use your leg, you'll feel your horse filling up the outside rein. Keep that rein close to his neck and withers, and slightly open your inside rein, as you ask for a little bend: just enough that you see the corner of his inside eye. The judge will see—will *expect* to see—your horse looking a little bit toward the inside of the ring.

As you start to play with positioning, you're going to find that tracking one way (whichever is your horse's naturally hollow direction), you need no inside rein at all. Tracking the other way (his stiffer direction), though, you'll have to ask for the bend quite actively. Do it! Ask as strongly as necessary to get the job done. But then—once again,

the left (outside) rein is *allowing*.

3. Passing the point of the corner, I want to get myself right on the track immediately next to the fence so I can establish at least one stride on the track before starting the diagonal. I'm already pointing Tucker's nose a little bit across the diagonal, but I've got to make sure . . .

4. . . . all four legs are cleanly ON the track between corner and diagonal—that's important. Tucker's nose is passing M; as I'm just starting to make the turn, I'm looking across to K. He's showing a solid bend—perhaps a tad more than necessary. Ideally, he should be looking almost at K, too.

(Continued on next page)

CORNER TO CORNER
(continued)

5. I've just left the track, still riding most of the bend I had in the turn. It's more bend than I need, but I made a strong effort to keep the bend through the turn.

6. A stride later, Tucker is straighter between my reins. This is the right amount of positioning for the diagonal: He's just slightly bent right, and my outside leg is just a tad back to maintain the "flat" bend to X.

7. We've just crossed X, and here's the new positioning to the left—his stiffer side, so he's brought his nose in more than his poll, a typical evasion to bending. My right leg is now slightly back, my left on the girth.

8. RIGHT: Instead of heading dead straight to K, I'm pointing Tucker to a spot a horse's length before it and keeping a little positioning left. (My heel is badly up!) I'll bend him more just before we step onto the track.

9. WRONG: Here's what happens when you aim at the letter. Tucker's nose may have come onto the track at K, but his body is a whole stride late!

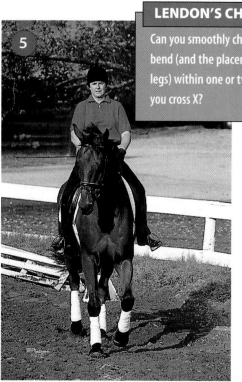

LENDON'S CHALLENGE

Can you smoothly change the bend (and the placement of your legs) within one or two strides as you cross X?

RIGHT

WRONG

and for as long as I teach, and forever and ever after that—*soften* for at least a few strides.

Another Little Geometry Lesson

Even with good positioning, you can mess up straight lines in the turns and corners—mostly because horses generally want to turn a little sooner and a little more than you ask them to. This is important because, as I explained in Lesson 20, a dressage arena is not made up of two straight lines connected by two 20-meter half-circles. It is made up of four straight lines connected by four corners (actually small quarter-circles); and you have to *show the judge all of them, all the time.* (How small the corners are depends on your horse's level of training and the gait he's in. Even at Training Level, you should be able to ride a fairly deep corner at the walk and a moderately deep corner at the trot. Depending on your control, at the canter you may ride something not significantly different from a 20-meter quarter-circle.)

How Corners Ruin Straight Lines

Let's say you're going down the track on the long side, from K to H. Your horse is nicely positioned right, but as early as S (the second letter from the corner), you start losing the track and your straightness. What's more, you lose any chance of riding a correct corner and, therefore, a *bona fide* short side.

Here's what the judge might see: You're looking around the corner. Your inside leg is passive, not pushing your horse toward the outside rein. He's lost his rightward positioning. And everything—including you, who might even be leaning—is drifting a little right.

My point: To complete the long side and ride a straight short side properly, you have to *make your horse go into the corner.* (Believe me, if you've been letting him "drift" through the short side all this time, a true corner is going to come as quite a shock. For help, see "Troubleshooting" on page 133.)

What's more, you have to start making him do it by S. That means:

• making sure he stays "positioned" right

• creating a sense with your whole body—including your eyes—of going straight out over the rail on the short side

• keeping your right leg at the girth to say, "You stay out here," and your left rein steady to tell his left shoulder, "Keep this out here, too." You're not pulling him left. You're half-halting with right leg and left rein to tell him, "Wait a minute; don't turn yet," so he doesn't fall in around the turn. Prepare as I'm describing, and by the time you arrive at H, the turn will practically happen on its own. You just have to figure out two things: How deep can you go without disrupting your horse's throughness, balance, and suppleness? And, with the straight short side coming up (which you're going to make yourself ride just that way: as a *straight, short* side), how strongly and how soon do your straightening aids have to happen to keep him from overturning off the track?

A horse isn't like a car; he can't react

THE WIDE VIEW . . .

1. . . . lets us see the rhythm. Tucker's flowing into the turn clearly positioned between all my bending aids, including right leg at the girth and a nice leading-type (not indirect) inside rein.

2. We stay close to the corner (the flowerpot being the point of this "corner"). It's obvious that I'm going to continue the turn onto the diagonal—because even though Tucker's legs are moving onto the track of the long side, we're both looking across the diagonal. I've positioned his head, and . . .

3. . . . as we start the diagonal, he's following where that head was positioned.

in a split second. He's always going to take another step. So stop your turning aids at least one stride before you want him to go straight. (More exact than "at least one" I cannot be. Horses aren't robots, I can't program them for you, and this is just stuff you have to practice and figure out.) Allow the last turning stride as you think and feel "dead straight ahead": Sit absolutely square, with your shoulders straight, and give a half-halt—squeeze your inside leg against the girth, and take a little on your outside rein—to say "No more turn."

Now excuse me for a moment while I climb up and survey the view from . . .

Lendon's Soapbox

A corner is not something you think about only in the show ring. A corner is not simply a pain-in-the-neck way to get from one straight line to another. A corner is *the best half-halting, aids-coordinating, suppling, engaging, balancing exercise you can do on a daily basis.* And every circuit of a dressage arena provides you with four such opportunities. A corner is a specific movement, as much

as a leg-yield or a canter pirouette is, so ride it with equal dedication, focus, and precision from now until the day you leave the arena for the last time.

Thank you!

Four Secrets of a Good Diagonal Line

Let's take M to X to K, for example:

1. Make one continuous turn from the short side to the long side to the diagonal line. There's just not enough room for a Training Level horse (unless he's really itty-bitty) to ride the corner, start down the long side, and then turn onto the diagonal—or turn off the diagonal, start down the long side, and ride a separate corner. Now, don't get me wrong: This is not carte blanche to cut corners. Quite the contrary: Your one continuous turn *must* include your clearly stepping on the track of the long side.

2. Look ahead. Eyeball the spot where you're going to meet the track at K before you turn off the track at M. (If you turn onto the diagonal line and then search for

LENDON'S CHALLENGE

Can you ride from C to A—corner, diagonal, corner—without any change in your horse's rhythm?

your point, rather than turning to your point, I guarantee you'll overshoot and have to overcorrect. That's always a mess.)

3. Position your horse by thinking of the diagonal as a very flat S. Before and through the corner, bend him around your strong inside (right) leg that's pushing him into your outside (left) connecting rein. As his nose comes to M, start to leave the track, keeping him very slightly positioned right to X. As you cross X, momentarily straighten him by leveling out all your aids. Then develop an itsy-bitsy left bend—left leg at the girth actively pushes him over toward your outside, filled-out, connecting right rein. To Joe Schmoe, he'll look basically straight throughout. To an expert—the judge, let's hope—he will be superbly positioned. To you, he'll be ready at K to flow seamlessly into the true, obvious bend of the corner. A good deal all around!

4. Aim to meet the track a horse's length before K—so you have plenty of time and space for a nice corner. A horse is a long creature. If you point his nose at K, by the time the rest of him arrives on the track and gets straight, he'll be a step or two beyond K and you'll have buried him in the corner (or he'll have saved his own bacon by cutting the corner, making you miss it entirely).

Troubleshooting

• If your horse has been allowed to "drift" through corners all this time, he's in the habit of sliding around the turn, leaning in, going on his forehand, and simply not going anywhere near the wall. You try the aids I'm giving you—inside leg and outside rein—but nothing much happens; he doesn't take the half-halt.

Time for a basic lesson: As you approach each corner, walk; firmly push your horse out into the corner. Trot the next side; walk in good time for the next corner, then push him out again, and so on. When he listens to your aids in the walk, try the trot—but as you approach each corner, *think* the aids for walk, so that you bring him back; then ride the corner. Actually walking, and then thinking the walk aids as you trot, will make your aids definite—and will discipline him to take the half-halt.

• If your horse falls on his inside shoulder and drifts in off the track, leg-yield him out (catch him as his weight starts to shift and you're talking an almost imperceptible half-step). And remember: Your reins do not change in a leg-yield (we don't call it a "rein-yield"!), so don't try to pull him back to the track with your outside rein. Keep that rein against his neck to create a sense of holding him from going further out.

• If your corners get sloppy because your long-side canter-trot transitions—between B and F, for example—are a little out of control, trot at or shortly past B so you have the rest of the long side to reposition and prepare for a smooth, flowing corner. (Then again, if your horse is very balanced and under control, trot *right before the corner* for a strategic bit of bravado and showmanship.)

• If your horse "ricochets" onto the diagonal line in his stiffer direction—let's say the right—so he bends left and falls right, school him all the way to X by keeping a very strong right leg at the girth (almost as if you're leg-yielding) and maintaining almost too much right bend. Not that this is what you want to do ultimately; it's just that he must not make that turn, take control, and throw his shoulders to the inside. ■

THE ENTRANCE

1. If I were the judge watching my student Marjaleena Berger and nine-year-old Lucas (a Danish Warmblood) enter the arena, I would score this as a very, very good center line. Lucas is centered in the gate and straight—you can barely see his hind legs, his nose is dead center on his

LENDON'S CHALLENGE

Can you maintain the exact same contact on both reins coming up the center line—so your horse stays absolutely straight and doesn't "ricochet" back and forth from rein to rein?

chest, and his ears are level. (Only a super-picky judge would complain about not seeing A exactly between the horse's legs when everything else looks so nice.) How did it happen? Marjaleena did a good job . . .

Straight Lines:
Center Line, Halt, Salute

NOW WE MOVE ON TO THE SECOND part of our focus on straight lines, including how to ride a perfectly straight center line, the halt, and the salute (including the one quality you and your horse need to demonstrate most at this level).

You'll Succeed If You . . .

• Start now to make precision a way of life—you cannot wait until the week before the show. Every single day, school straight center lines, even if they're just to get to the other ring, or from the oak tree to the maple tree, or from this rock to that dandelion. And when you halt, halt *exactly* at that letter or this post or that jump standard.

• Develop a brisk, businesslike, military-type salute—not a cute, fluttery little "Gee, Judge, hi there," but a proud "I am here. I am ready. I am d----ed good!" That's the look that'll get the judge in the right state of mind for your test.

• Know what you can live with. If your horse doesn't halt well on the bit, work on it; but don't drill and drill and drill to the point of making him defensive. Don't put bright-red flashing lights on the fact by sitting at X, sawing on his mouth, and bending him this way and that. (With no forward motion for your hands to connect to, you're only going to get a fight anyway.) Just pretend that he's exactly where you want him. Then get out of there quickly, gracefully, and with as little fuss and bother as possible, so you can put him back on the bit with one of the many tools I've already given you—a little vibrating wiggle, say—and make the rest of your test wonderful.

• Develop defensive aids. Most horses tend to repeat the same evasions and resistances. Say, for example, your horse always

2. . . . outside the ring: She started the rather sharp turn into the ring by looking down the center line and bending her horse left, her left leg on his side (though it could have been closer to the girth to lessen her risk of pushing his haunches out to the right) and her left hand asking for a little bend. We can't see her outside right hand or leg, but we can sure tell they were creating the nice, spongy wall she needed to keep him from drifting right. All this put them on line for the entrance we saw in photo 1. Now she just has to maintain everything by making . . .

3. . . . absolutely no change in her hand or leg aids, and Lucas stays straight right into the halt.

THE HALT

1. Practicing at home, Marjaleena finds that Lucas (a big, powerful mover) needs a lot of support to whoa. She gives a fairly dramatic half-halt, even momentarily bringing her upper body behind the vertical, and he responds obediently by shifting his weight back and putting on the brakes. But—in a fairly typical moment for Training Level—he also comes a little against her hand and in front of the bit. Tactfully, she doesn't keep pulling or ask any more firmly. As a result . . .

2. . . . Lucas melts into a very nice walk (remember, walk steps are permitted and even expected at this level) with his head down and barely in front of the vertical. This is a good Training Level frame and a nice straight center line. Lucas is on the bit, accepting the aids, and not scrunched together; Marjaleena is doing her part by looking straight ahead. (A quibbler might say her chin is down just a bit.)

LENDON'S CHALLENGE

Can you halt without your horse's pressure on the bit changing? Can you even give your hand forward a little, so he comes back in response to your weight alone?

throws his haunches left when he halts. Have Great-Aunt Gertie watch your transition to make sure he's not actually bulging his shoulders right (a very different evasion that may end up looking like "haunches left"). After two or three repeat-problem halts, you should not only know what he's going to do but know which "defensive" aid or aids you need to catch him beforehand (in this case, sliding your left leg back a little more)—and put them to use.

The Center Line: Straight Is the Name of the Game

I've talked a lot in these pages about "positioning" your horse with a teeny-tiny inside bend. But this is the one instance in which you want him to be absolutely straight, with his nose centered right between the points of his shoulders.

Ideally, the best way to *keep* him straight (and to ride a straight center line without weaving and overcorrecting) is to sit absolutely square on his back and stay eyeball-to-eyeball with the judge from the moment you turn onto the center line until the moment you turn off it. But what if your horse—like every horse in the world—is naturally hollow on one side: to the left, say, so he always tends to drift ever-so-slightly right? Keep him on the center line and appearing straight by imperceptibly bending him right so he drifts left, away from the bend (in part because his shoulders are going that way and in part because your strong right leg is on the girth).

3. A stride later, she can subside her aids into the very light contact that will . . .

4. . . . . give her the best possible shot at a good halt. (Pulling the whole way would only make the halt very resistant.)

5. And here we are! Lucas may not be 100 percent square (his left legs are probably 2 or 3 inches farther back than they should be)—but pulllease! I'll never get hung up about a Training Level horse being only 98 percent square if he's also standing in a lovely frame with his nose a little in front of the vertical, his neck out in front of him, good contact on the bit, and his four legs under him. To me, that *is* square.

THE SALUTE

1. The big deal here is for Marjaleena to bridge the reins and salute without losing her contact or upsetting Lucas's equilibrium. Here's how she does it: Holding the left rein between her left thumb and forefinger, she opens her other left fingers. Keeping contact on the right rein, she moves her right hand, rein, and whip toward the left.

2. In the very next moment, she opens her right hand to release the rein and whip and . . .

3. . . . . takes them in her left.

4. With her left hand now holding everything and keeping the unbroken connection, Marjaleena stays balanced, straight, and centered as she drops her right hand straight down behind her thigh, its back facing the judge and her fingers softly closed. Then she very simply nods her chin down and back up again. (No-no's? Turning your palm forward as if you were begging, or leaving your chin down so you look as if you're snapping your neck off.)

The Halt: The Straighter the Better

And the best way to stay straight? Halt gradually. No—let me put it another way: The best way to make your horse crooked is to ask him to halt more abruptly than he's able to. Fortunately, at Training Level you are allowed—you are *expected*—to have a few walk steps between your trot and

your halt. So start now to experiment with how many steps he takes from the moment you ask until you're immobile. Do it this way:

As soon as you're established on the center line, give a tiny little half-halt to make sure your horse is "come-backable" and listening, and to tell him a halt is coming and not to be surprised. (Surprise is the

LENDON'S CHALLENGE

Can you bridge your reins, make your salute, and return the reins to two hands without having your horse anticipate, drop the bit, or change in any way?

main ingredient in a bad halt.)

If he feels straight, close your legs and bring them evenly back a few inches—not to push his haunches somewhere, but to keep them from going anywhere.

If he's NOT straight—say he's hollow to the left with his shoulders to the right—bend him right with your right leg at the girth and your right rein.

If he starts to go against the bit, close your legs more and vibrate or slide the bit a little left and right to ask him to come a teensy bit deep.

To ask your horse to halt, sit a little bit deeper and then ask for a half-halt: Momentarily—for no more than a stride—take straight back on both reins; then subside your aids. If he's green, you may need to apply a series of half-halts, momentarily asking him to come back and immediately subsiding your aids, asking again and subsiding, until he halts.

What mostly happens is that you ask once with a half-halt (and subside), your horse starts to come back, you can feel he's going to continue coming back, and you don't have to ask again. He knows the halt; he just needs a couple of steps to get the whole thing done.

Ideally—and this will take some time—the halt happens without your using your hands at all: You simply stop following the motion, sit deep, and he melts into the halt. (Most important of all, don't just continuously pull on his mouth until he's halted. The result won't be attractive!)

Just as you feel your horse is about to halt, square him up in front with another half-step, either squeezing your legs to ask or backing off your hand to allow. (Never try to square him up by backing; the worst sin in the halt is stepping back. You always want him thinking "forward.")

And don't sweat the small stuff. Re-member, although it's easy for the judge at C to tell if you're off the center line, it's very difficult to tell whether you are absolutely between B and E. My point: Make a smooth, very straight, very balanced halt, and if you're a stride early or a stride late—no problem.

The Salute: Immobility Counts

In the halt, your horse must be straight. His weight must be on all four legs. He must be square, or close to it, in front. (At this level, he's probably not enough on your aids that he'll *always* be square behind. But if he's dead straight in front, the judge can't see his hind legs anyway—and will have no idea if he's square behind or not.) Above all, he must be absolutely immobile.

So practice standing. Stand there for thirty seconds. Look around. Scratch your nose. Drop the reins; pick up the reins. To salute, maintain contact while placing the reins (and your whip) in your left hand—put the right rein in your left hand and take the whip with your left thumb; then drop your right hand (palm rearward) and quietly nod your head. (For more on the salute, see the photos at left.) Take the reins in both hands again. Practice this to the point where you can do it without your horse so much as flicking an ear.

Teach him to wait. Keep your legs "there" at all times. If he steps back, check that you're not holding or pulling back, and close your leg to say "NO!" If he creeps forward, give him a half-halt. If he fidgets (and let's hope you didn't teach him to fidget by over-trying to square him up), try to relax him. Pat him and tell him he's wonderful. And don't ask him to stand when it's not going to work—the bugs are horrendous or everybody else has left the ring—because, again, you'll just teach him to fidget. ■

TURN OFF THE CENTER LINE AT C

1. Lucas must have moved out of the halt straight, on the bit, and in a nice forward tempo—because Marjaleena is clearly not making any kind of adjustment. As he approaches C, she prepares him to follow his nose around the turn to the right: She puts her right leg very definitely on his body at the girth and creates a slight right bend with her rein.

LENDON'S CHALLENGE

Can you stay absolutely straight on the center line, without drifting, until you actually start to step in the direction of the turn?

2. In the next stride, Lucas starts the turn, bringing his front legs a little bit right and keeping his face on the vertical—which tells me that even as Marjaleena asks for the right bend, she's allowing it with her left rein.

3. One stride later, his front feet are about to reach the track, his hind feet are coming off the center line, he's showing good bend, and his haunches are following his forehand—that right hind is just about to land in the print

LESSON 23

Turns Off and Onto Center Line

OK, WE'VE GOTTEN YOU INTO THE dressage arena and up the center line for a nice square halt at X and a snappy salute. Now you'll continue learning how to knock the socks off the judge with . . .

• a brisk, energetic, straight move-off from the halt at X (including tips on how to do it so your horse doesn't lurch, wander, or drift left or right)

• an accurate turn off the center line at C (a turn that's straight like a dressage horse's, not swervy like a hunter's)

• and a balanced and precise turn onto the center line at A: one that doesn't go wide and overshoot by a mile.

To begin, let me remind you that you . . .

Never Give Points Away

Turns off and onto the center line are super-tight for a Training Level horse, especially if he's a big mover. (You don't get to full 10-meter circles until Second Level, when your horse is collected and much better balanced and on the aids.) But c'mon, guys: The fact that these turns are tight doesn't mean they can't be done. And it doesn't mean the judge is going to look the other way and not penalize you if you shamble through one. You should—you can—make yourself do them right. And you can—and should—do them right the first time and every time.

OK, OK. I'll give you one practice turn each. Go wide, go late, go skidding around the corner on two legs. After that, I don't want to see it any more. You don't get "do-overs" in a dressage test, and you won't get them from me. Get out there, get your rear in gear—and the next time, turn too early!!

You'll Succeed If You . . .

• Move off from X with a purpose, as if you want to attack the judge, run him over, or ride your horse right down his throat!

• Ride the turn onto the center line exactly the way you ride the turn off the center line.

of his right fore. From hip to heel, Marjaleena's leg is so close it's practically wrapped around his belly; her shoulders are following his shoulders and his placement, and everything looks very balanced. But even so, with such a big guy at Training Level, there's no way she can pull off a corner/straight-line/corner short side. So . . .

4. . . . she makes a flowing U-turn instead, allowing him to touch just one clear stride on the short-side track. Only one thing mars this picture: Instead of looking down the long side, where she's going, Marjaleena's looking at where her horse is.

4

TURN ONTO THE CENTER LINE AT A

1. Again, when you have a big, powerful Training Level horse trying to negotiate such a relatively tight turn (and—let's face it—complete it accurately without the support of the rail), you have to help him maintain balance and the quality of the trot by riding a U-turn, rather than a corner/ straight-side/corner. Marjaleena shows us she's going to do just that by setting up the turn on the long side: She stays there as long as possible, looks around the corner to where she wants to go, and "positions" Lucas right by pressing her inside (right) leg at the girth and elastically asking with her right hand. (You can see the rein is well off his neck.)

2. Halfway through the turn, she's created just a bit more right bend with her right leg still very strongly on the girth, her right rein still asking for the right bend, and her left hand close to the withers in support. Lucas touches the short side for one stride as she continues

Make the corner as deep as you can without losing the rhythm or tempo of the trot, and use your outside leg and rein as a "wall."

• Realize, when your horse tends to get a little out of control barreling down the long side after the canter, that you'll make that turn onto the center line only if you come to the trot early and you do something about slowing his tempo and shortening his stride.

• Put poles or cones on the ground to keep from swerving wide at C or overshooting A. Better yet, have Great-Aunt Gertie stand there; you won't want to run over her. (I can't tell you how many times I've gotten so frustrated with some BOZO who's already turned late twenty-five times in a row that I've risked life and limb by placing my body on the center line.

Fortunately, apparently no one's ever been quite ready to kill me—and they suddenly figure out how to make the turn just fine.)

• Try harder! The biggest reason—pure and simple—that people swerve wide when they turn off the center line at C, or that they don't turn onto the center line at A in time, is that they don't try hard enough!

The Move-Off: Go to the Judge

We pick up where we stopped in Lesson 22: Your horse is halted, and you've just finished your salute. Now close your legs (don't suddenly swing them back and clamp him in the ribs) and ask him to trot briskly ahead, because forward energy—combined with your eyeball-to-eyeball focus—is what will make him straight. (If, by the way, you really blew your halt and

LENDON'S CHALLENGE

Can you ride the turn with absolutely no change in tempo or rhythm?

ended up 5 feet off the center line, don't do a lot of turns and zigzags to get back on it. Simply ride straight to the judge from there.)

Turn Off the Center Line at C

Let's say that, in the test you're riding, the turn is to the right. The trick is to establish a little bit of a suppling right bend on the center line—and when to do this very much depends on your horse and whether the turn is toward his hollow or his stiff side.

Does he like to drift to the left? From the moment you leave X, bend him left with your left leg on the girth. Change to a right bend as late as you can: Bring your right leg onto the girth, and slide your left leg behind the girth to keep him from falling out to the left as he makes the turn.

(How much inside versus outside leg? I can't tell you. That's up to you and your horse.)

One last thing: Don't come straight down the center line, get your right bend for the turn, and then make a funny little drift to the left. I know, in the hunter world we were all taught to use all the space available to make our turns easier. But here we're trying to show off a straight center line and a balanced turn, so don't do it!

Turn Onto the Center Line at A: Make a U-Turn!

As I mentioned a little earlier, this half-a-10-meter-circle turn is tight for a Training Level horse, especially with no wall to support you on the "landing side." And if he's a young, big-moving thing who's not incredibly well balanced or on the aids, he's probably barreling along a little bit out of control

to look directly down the center line; her eyes tell you exactly where she is and where she's going.

3. Two more steps and Lucas is halfway between short side and center line. He still has a nice bend and his face is pretty much vertical; in fact, everything—position, rhythm, power—is just a continuation of what he had on the long side. Note, by the way, that Marjaleena's headed toward the center line so far ahead of A that you can't even see the letter yet. Continuing on this U-turn line . . .

4. . . . will (next page) bring them dead smack onto the center line, still moving in that powerful, rhythmic-looking trot—Marjaleena never had to bring him back to the tiny, mincey steps he would have needed for a less well-planned turn. His hind feet are a bit to the inside, and he's still got a right bend, but she's thinking about straightening him. In one more stride, he'll be per-

TURN ONTO THE CENTER LINE AT A
(continued)

fectly straight and straddling A. She's still looking beautifully ahead to . . .

5. . . . a perfect finish on the center line. You could say that Lucas's nose isn't quite centered on his chest (he's still very lightly positioned right, with his jaw giving a little rightward), but that hasn't disrupted his balance in any way. As far as we—and the judge!—can tell, he's so well aligned that he's got only forelegs, with A pretty much centered between them.

after his canter. What's more, the judge sitting at C can tell almost to the millimeter whether you arrive on the center line early, dead-on, or late.

Those are the perils. How to avoid them? Say you're tracking right at F . . .

• Practice with ground poles marking the center line until you get the hang of the geometry.

• Get your trot early enough on the long side to whoa, bring your horse back a little, and shorten his stride—because the slower he's going, the easier the turn will be to navigate.

• Turn your head at F and look at the center line. As you turn onto the short side, look over your shoulder. From then on, maintain eyeball-to-eyeball contact with the judge.

• Ride the turn as a 10-meter U-turn: Leave the rail a stride or so past F (the farther you go into the corner for the first

half, the more room you'll have for the second half), touching the short-side track for one stride and arriving right on the center line about 5 meters up from A.

• Use your outside rein and leg as a "wall" to keep your horse from bulging out.

• Don't ride the turn as a corner, straight line, and corner—unless your horse is small and/or very well balanced and supple.

• Don't cut the corner between the long side and the short side—you'll make the turn from the short side to the center line that much sharper.

• Don't turn more than 180 degrees (you'll really look disorganized trying to weave your way back to the center line).

• Don't go beyond the center line, because there's no way to cover that up. Err, if you must, by being early and gently drifting out, so you look as if your turn was just a little too shallow. ■

Medium to Free Walk— and Back to Medium

MEDIUM TO FREE WALK ON A LOOSE REIN

1. Sancho Panza (a Lusitano cross) and Marjaleena are coming very much into the corner, just the way you'd like them to at the medium walk. (You'd expect less deepness at the trot and even less at the canter.) Sancho's relaxed and on the bit; and with Marjaleena's right leg well on the girth to help him bend right, he's very well aligned through his body.

2. Ah, the value (next page) of preparation! Coming through the corner, Marjaleena looks across the diagonal toward M, marches Sancho well forward, and relaxes her fingers just enough to let the reins slide a tad, encouraging him to lengthen his stride and start stretching forward and down. The result? He's definitely on the bit and in a medium walk, but in a longer-necked frame and a little less connected. In the next stride, she can open her fingers and let the reins

slide even more, and he'll show a clear beginning to the free walk at K. Sure enough . . .

3. . . . leaving K and heading across the diagonal, he's in a beautiful, long-strided free walk (see how the reach of his hind legs forms a big triangle?), with his neck well on its way to stretching down. Why, you ask, is the right rein looser than the left? Marjaleena's either encouraging the stretch by easing one rein more than the other or making the tiniest bit of correction to his line toward M—and rightly so: If she doesn't establish that diagonal line in the first stride off the track, Sancho will drift— and she'll have unattractive major adjustments to make farther on.

4. I call this "giving a horse all the rein he'll take plus an inch more, but not suicide" reins. Sancho's got all the freedom he needs to stretch down in an unquestionably free walk, but Marjaleena can still make a quick little adjustment should he wander or lose his focus. Her eyes are lasered on M, and her hands are in a normal, correct, low position. (She's not

I'VE PUT OFF THIS "DECEPTIVELY simple" movement until now because it's the one you're most likely to mess up if the other pieces—corners, straight lines, accuracy, responsiveness—aren't in place. But . . .

It's No Cause for Panic
After all, you're no stranger to the walk. When we started these lessons, one of the first things I had you work on was stabilization: teaching your horse to maintain any gait—walk included—at any speed until he

hears otherwise from you. Since then, we've done or begun many of our little exercises at the walk—yielding to hand and leg, walking the square, coming on the aids, stretching forward and down. Most recently, we've zeroed in on navigating circles, corners, and straight lines. Because all those pieces should be pretty solid, now all we really have to do with the medium to free to medium walk is make sure it works for you in the ring. (If the underlying

LENDON'S CHALLENGE

Can you get your horse—gradually and continuously—to stretch down and maintain a powerful push from behind?

Free Walk on a Long Rein—Maintaining Contact

Which is better in the free walk: a loose rein or a long rein? The answer depends on you and your horse—on such factors as whether he's young or green. All the judge wants to see is a stretch like Sancho's here—where, even though Marjaleena's got a definite, very even contact on both reins, his poll is lower than his withers and there's no sense of contraction in his neck.

letting the reins go loose with her fingers but untrustingly raising her hands to maintain contact.) And even though she's on a loose rein, her fairly long arms allow her to follow the motion of his neck and maintain the same amount of feel throughout the stride, instead of going loose, taut, loose, taut, loose.

5. Here's a great sequence. Very often, when you give the rein, your horse will stretch only until he hits the rein and stops. But just as Sancho runs into the rein and regains contact, Marjaleena . . .

6. . . . gives him a little bit more. He responds by going so much lower (the line of his neck is a little below horizontal, his poll slightly lower than his withers) that she actually has to reach down. What a pleasant picture that makes, with him projecting an almost palpable air of relaxation and showing us a verrrry long stride—look at the spread between his hind legs!

stuff isn't solid, either there's a hole in what you've already done—and, let's face it, part of dressage is uncovering those little holes—or you're still struggling with doing movements at a precise spot instead of when you feel ready. Retrace your steps to discover and fill in the gaps. Or, if readiness is the issue, forge ahead—because practice makes perfect!)

Your Goal . . .

. . . is to—seamlessly, and when and where it's called for—

• Go from working trot to your biggest, longest on-the-aids walk in a nice, round frame that's "connected" but in no way restricted.

• Go to a free walk that's just what the name says: your biggest, longest possible walk, on a completely loose (though not flapping on-the-buckle) rein that gives your horse total freedom to lower his neck and extend his nose into the stretchiest frame he can give you. If he's so young or green that he drifts and wanders, you may need to maintain a very light contact—but still on a long rein, and just enough to steer without restricting. To me, the best free walk feels as if I'm on the verge of no control, except that I can trust my horse not to jig, get distracted and throw his head in the air, or wander.

• Return to the medium walk by very gradually and softly gathering up the reins so your horse just "melts" back into your hands with a more connected, slightly more controlled (but neither slower nor shorter) walk that still has the very forward attitude you need to . . .

• Pull off the upcoming trot transition—and, in some cases, the almost-immediate canter.

FREE WALK TO MEDIUM WALK

1. Sancho's still totally off contact and in a nice free walk as he and Marjaleena approach the end of the diagonal, but she's already looking ahead and thinking about getting her act back together.

2. Without changing his walk in any way, she makes the first step toward reestablishing contact by taking a light feel on the inside left rein. (The right rein, you can see, is still slightly loose.)

3. Now she's established contact on the right rein as well. Sancho's stride is still big, but he's accepting the bit (although he's not yet *on* the bit) and bringing his head up in a very nice way. What I very much like about this moment is that Marjaleena's arms are still well out in front of her. She hasn't done what so many people do to shorten the reins: bring their arms back, an option that stops working when their arms can't go back any farther.

4. With K one stride away, Sancho's in the same carriage, with the same height of neck, but he's starting to come together and show a little

It's Lendon's Soapbox Time

Listen! You have no excuse for getting a low score on this movement unless your horse's walk is so God-given poor that—but wait a minute. There's almost no walk so bad you can't manage at least a 6 as long as you practice, practice, practice by . . .

• experimenting. I can't tell you how much leg you'll

LENDON'S CHALLENGE

Can you take your horse from stretching down to melting back into contact and on the aids in one fluid, uninterrupted, upward line, without his throwing his head up or inverting in any way?

need to produce an energetic walk. Is your horse naturally forward-going? Is he naturally sluggish? If you kick, kick, kick, does he break to the trot, or does he puff up against you and resist? When you come to the medium walk from the free walk, is he cranky because he thought he was done for the day? This is stuff you need to know.

• keeping your loose-reined, free-walking horse on the straight and narrow by looking ahead (it's amazing how a horse will follow your eyes) and controlling him with your legs. If he starts to drift right, for example, find out just how much right leg is enough to set up a "wall" but not make him leg-yield. (Again, if he drifts and wanders because he's green, you may need a *touch* of contact, but just enough to steer and not restrict.)

• gradually and smoothly shortening your reins as you go from free to medium walk; figuring out how many strides you'll need to take so you end up in medium walk precisely at the letter; keeping the connection so your horse doesn't throw his head in the air; testing, during this transition, how strong your leg has to be to maintain forward energy and "position" in the "teeny-tiny, itsy-bitsy inside bend" I talked about in Lesson 21, and how light it has to be to keep him from jigging.

• regularly asking for an energetic free walk at home. Make it your credo that the walk (any walk, any time you walk) is not the gait of taking a break, giving your horse the reins, and resting. Why? Because otherwise, how, in a test, will he know he's not supposed to snatch the reins out of your hands, stare at the geese flying overhead, or stall out? Start today making every step of walk the very best, and marching forward will become his way of life. And that's the quality that will lead to a good score in your tests.

Now that we've got our thinking laid out, let's try the movement from Training Level Test 1. Tracking left, you go from working canter to working trot between B and M, to medium walk at C, to free walk across the diagonal (H to X to F), to medium walk at F, and to working trot at A.

Working Trot to Medium Walk

At this level, the judge is looking for a soft, forward transition at the letter, meaning that the first walk step must happen as your horse passes C. How far before C you ask to accomplish that depends on his "come-backability" (which you should know from experimentation) and the way he's responding at the moment (test with half-halts to find out). If you wait to ask at C or a stride

flexion. His face is nearly on the vertical, and his stride is very slightly shorter (although it's still very big and he's still a very forward-looking horse). I wish his mouth wasn't slightly open, but that has nothing to do with Marjaleena's pulling him together (note that the rein is neither tight nor hard). This tendency to pull his tongue up and open his mouth a little is just a minor Sancho idiosyncrasy.

5. Marjaleena arrives at K already looking around the corner to the left, with her left leg closed and Sancho in a very slightly shorter-strided walk and a little bit of a frame. He's accepting the soft contact (even though he's still playing with his tongue); and because Marjaleena never tried to shorten his stride, it happened all by itself. The result . . .

6. . . . as he bends around the corner, is that his good, long stride is exactly where it should be—in an energetic, forward-moving, Training Level medium walk.

HOW TO MAINTAIN CONTACT AS YOU SHORTEN REIN

1. Reach your right hand across toward your left. Without releasing the right rein, grip the left rein between your right thumb and forefinger. Open the fingers of your left hand and . . .

2. . . . . slide that hand down the rein toward your horse's mouth, to where you can establish contact.

3. The number-one duty of your left hand now is to neither abuse nor abandon your horse's mouth, so maintain that contact as you squeeze the right rein between your left thumb and forefinger and . . .

4. . . . . slide your right hand down the rein toward his mouth until you can establish contact there as well.

before, you'll be late. If you rip his mouth out in desperation, you may be accurate, but you'll have an ugly, baaaaad transition. Instead, start thinking about the transition as you're cantering down the long side toward B. If your horse is very "come-backable," show off by waiting a bit longer; but if he likes to run on a bit, trotting at or immediately after B will give you plenty of time and space to gain control. (If he's very unresponsive, you may have to do something

resembling a very long canter-walk transition, where you literally trot and ask for the walk at B and continue asking down the long side and through the corner.)

In any event, as soon as you trot, tune in your sensors to his responsiveness by asking him to slow a stride: Half-halt on the outside rein (again, how much half-halt is up to you and him); then ask, "What is the feeling in my hand? How much horse have I got? How big is his stride? Is he running

LENDON'S CHALLENGE

Once you've established contact with one rein, can you maintain it and not go "loose, tight, loose, tight"?

on a bit or just going nicely forward?"

If your horse barrels ahead on his fore-hand, you've got room to work with. If he comes right back, you can trot to and even around the corner before asking for the walk—the ideal situation if you ride the corner well, because you can use the corner to balance him for the transition. (Remember that his ridability also affects the deepness of your corner. If he's running away with you, going deep will either bury him or make him jump the rail and leave the arena.)

Then ask for the walk transition by sitting a few strides if you've been posting (an option in Training Level Test 1 or 2), keeping your legs very close and using take-and-give half-halts so that from the first step his stride is forward, purposeful, and marching. (If you pull, pull, pull, pull, he'll dive, stall out, or pick up what I call a "funeral" walk.)

Medium Walk to Free Walk

Maintain a slight leftward position with your inside leg and rein, and ride a bit deeper into the corner than you would in trot. Use the one or two strides coming out of the corner toward H to firmly fix your eyeballs on F and relax your fingers enough to allow the reins to slide. Encourage your horse to stretch by following his motion (but without driving or grinding your seat into his back) and giving him all the rein he'll take plus about an inch more (unless—again—he's so green that he wanders or gawks at the cows across the field). He should be stretching into the free walk by the time you pass H and turn to cross the diagonal.

Free Walk to Medium Walk

As you approach the end of the diagonal, the big deal is to shorten your reins in such a gradual, subtle, tactful way that your horse just "melts" into your hands and returns to a more connected frame without fuss, bother, or change of rhythm or stride by the time his nose arrives at F. My recommendations:

• Start your shortening by establishing the new inside (right) bend and connection (which will also discourage head-throwing).

• Do it by closing your right leg on his side, pinching the right rein between your left thumb and forefinger, and sliding your right hand down the rein a bit—as shown at left. (Do not "walk up the reins" by wiggling and crawling your fingers along them like caterpillars, which would make keeping a feel of his mouth almost impossible.)

• Don't try to shorten all at once. Take two or three strides (and alternating reins) to imperceptibly bring your horse back on the aids.

Horses Don't Lie

If your horse goes from stretching down to "above the bit" before coming on the bit, he's telling me—and the judge at C—that you pull his head down into an artificial "head set," rather than moving him forward from leg to hand and getting him "on the aids." If he jigs, he's telling me that (on a day-to-day basis) after you walk around on a loose rein, you pick up the reins and immediately go to trot or canter, without first establishing a correct medium walk. You've trained him to think that as soon as the reins aren't loose, he's gonna do something.

In either case, he's bringing you back to my theme of the day: PRACTICE AT HOME! ■

> "As you approach the end of the diagonal, the big deal is to shorten your reins in such a gradual, subtle, tactful way that your horse just melts into your hands."

RIDE WITH PEOPLE WATCHING

My student Kerrie March, who's never shown, is practicing her test Under Pressure of People Watching: riding Sunstorm in front of (from left) actress Glenn Close (first time as an extra!) on Brian, Efraim Guevara, his brother Lupe (sitting), Johony Beltran, "Great-Aunt Gertie" (aka Jean Pacchiana), and Shane Crolick. Sunstorm's in a nice Training Level frame, active and forward, and Kerrie is sitting the trot pretty well, though she's being bounced back just a little—not unusual with a green rider on a bouncy horse.

Show Prep:
Ride a Whole Test!

WELL, MY FRIENDS, WE'VE ARRIVED at the moment when you gather up all the transitions and movements and figures we've been working on and string them together into a smooth, flowing, five- or six-minute-long Training Level test.

What the Heck Is the Big Deal . . .

. . . about riding a test without stops, do-overs, or *whenever-you're-readys*? Test riding is not about schooling. It's about showing off your horse. To do that, you have to know exactly what you and he can and can't do. And the only way to figure *that* out is to practice, practice, practice your test until you not only know where you're

going but know how and when you have to make little adjustments that become a part of memorizing your test—"OK, I do a trot circle at E and a canter transition at K, but I also know that crossing the center line I need to give him a little poke with my spur to keep him bent, approaching the rail I have to shoot him forward a bit, and on the long side toward K I have to soften that right side that's getting a little tough."

Why So Much Detail?

I want you to look forward to show day. I want you to know you're prepared the best you can be. I don't mean you couldn't be prepared better; I mean you and I know you've done everything you can do (given

PRACTICE IN A PLATOON OF HORSES

Before you go to a show, make sure you and your horse are both comfortable riding in a group. If you have to, invite all your neighbors over to ride with you and help you learn to take care of yourself, to watch out for the other rider, and to not get in the way of other people. Here we've staged a typical situation: One rider (me) is in the middle of the ring, starting to work on piaffe; students Courtney King and Kerrie, both working on the rail, are correctly passing left shoulder to left shoulder. Our green horse and rider are handling the situation very nicely, and everybody's looking ahead, trying to leave as much space as possible between horses. Looking ahead lets you see not only where other riders are and where you're going, but where *they're* going, too, so you don't suddenly cut in front of them. And they see where *you're* going, so they can stay out of your way.

FIX PROBLEMS IN "GRAY AREAS"

1. Most judges either can't see the corners of the dressage ring or don't look there. At home, I use the corners as a place to really put my horse on the aids and tell him, "Hey, I'm up here!" Then, if I need to, at a show I can use the corner to put him "extra-together." Here, for instance, cantering down the long side to H, Idocus has become very inattentive, looking off in the distance and coming way above my hand.

2. Within the next stride I've given him a half-halt: I've sat into him a little more and closed my aids together—leg on to keep him thinking and coming forward, bending a little to the right, left rein asking him to yield—and he's closed the door on his inattention and come right back to me. With another horse I might have had to set my hand for a split second, sliding the bit a little in his mouth (as we've talked about) to encourage him to come down. But even Idocus also has to get the message that "I don't want you to do that again"—in a show ring there'll always be something off the end of the

the fact that you're a mom with four kids, or you have a fourteen-hour-a-day desk job, or your horse has a sewing-machine trot). *That's* being ready to compete.

One other point: For Training Level at a one-day show, plan to ride three tests. The first will be a mess because you're late, you go to the wrong ring, or you blank out and go off course. In the second, you'll start to get things together. And by the third, you'll actually be breathing, thinking, and having fun!

But My Horse Will Memorize the Test!

I can't tell you how many people tell me that's why they don't practice tests. BUNK! If you show enough, your horse is going to memorize his tests anyway. (You can't show me a seasoned dressage horse who doesn't know he halts at X when he goes down center line.) The antidote for his learning the pattern and anticipating? Keep him waiting and "on the aids." School individual movements in a way that tells him, "We

don't *always* do that pattern. We do other things. Wait for me and I'll tell you what they're going to be."

For example, come down the center line, "threaten" to halt—and when he starts to slam on the brakes or get ahead of you, go forward and either halt somewhere else or don't halt at all. If he knows you always trot from the canter near the end of the long side, think about trotting, then change your mind and canter through the short side! If he jigs when you pick up your reins at the end of the free-walk diagonal, make certain during your daily sessions that you do *not* trot or canter as soon as you gather up your reins. And during a test, use a little trick that works for me because my horses are so well tuned to voice aids: Hum—sort of like "hmmmm-hmmm"—to settle him. The judge won't hear it. Even if he does, he won't believe it!

Practice Your Warm-Up, Too

We'll get into this in more detail in Lesson 26, when I help you warm up at the show, but now is the time to start figuring out when your horse is warmed up enough that he's ready to do his best work in a test. Again, this is not about making him better; it's about getting him to where he does everything he can do to the best of your mutual ability.

The movements, he already knows how to do (and if he always does a good halt, you don't need to—you shouldn't—practice ten of them anyway). So use your test-riding warm-up to learn how best to develop his gaits and responses. Get him alert. Get him to whoa and go. Get him a little settled, a little supple, and a little responsive. Stretch a little, do a few transitions, supple him left and right, maybe do a little gallop if he needs to think forward and

"yeehaw," or a little slow and quiet and long and low if he needs to settle. At Training Level, that's it! He should be ready to ride a test in ten or fifteen minutes.

What Riding a Whole Test Teaches You

• Get it right the first time. Why do some people school a canter depart ten times before getting it and others make sure it happens correctly the first time? The difference is frame of mind—what I call a "focused and disciplined test-riding mentality." Just erase from your mind the idea that you get freebies, or that anybody cares if "it always takes me two or three times to remind him not to put his head in the air during that transition." Figure out what you create the third time you ask that makes what you want happen. Now create it the first time!

And remember: An "I will make it work" attitude is clear-minded and effective but never angry. You can always say—rather firmly, I might add—"You are NOT going to do this to me again, you twerp!" But saying "Why are you doing this to me, you dirty, rotten horse?" means you're in trouble. Better to forget it and go on a loose rein— even in the middle of a practice test—until any whiff of anger is gone.

• Plan ahead. It is one thing to be trotting around the ring saying, "OK, I'm going to turn down the center line," and quite another to do your canter work, come to trot near the end of the long side, and immediately make a controlled, balanced, accurate turn down the center line. Your canter may have made your trot a bit strong, your horse may have gotten a bit heavy, and he may be a bit surprised by this "turn" of events. Constantly ask yourself, "Where am I going next? What do I have to do while I'm cantering a circle at C to make

long side to look at (horse trailers, horses working, deer coming out of the woods—you name it). So . . .

3. . . . . I begin getting ready to use the upcoming corner to overdiscipline him just a little, asking him to come a little too deep, too much together; getting his attention totally on me by putting his neck down and saying, "You do not put your head up in the air and look off into the distance."

4. I've really squished him deeply into this corner, bending him quite a bit; and I've set my hand again, just for a split second, making him too short in the neck and too deep, telling him "you *vill* pay attention!" Right after this, if I'm successful, I'll be able to allow him to go across the short side in a nice canter. And, yes, this is a little too much to do in a test— but most judges don't penalize what goes on in the corner if it isn't too obvious. And it sets up the rest of the test so he does not come way above the bit a second time! By sacrificing one point here, I may gain several in the rest of the test.

my long-side trot transition happen precisely at E? What do I have to do in the trot to keep him light and responsive and ready for the center line when it comes?" Consistently think about how what you're doing now affects things two movements ahead, and you'll be beating me—a lot!

• Use "gray areas." You can do a lot of fixing in corners and on short sides and on parts of the long side that seem to go on forever. If your horse is getting strong, for example, "over-slow" him in the corner. If he's getting lazy, send him forward with your spur or a touch of the whip on the short side. And use a mega-half-halt on that never-ending long side (preferably heading away from the judge) to say, "Come back here." Whatever you do, don't go catatonic and just try to get to the end (by which time your horse will be either pulling your arms out of your sockets or crawling along at 3 inches per hour). Even when you're not in a gray area, tell yourself, "If I let this continue, I'm lost. I need to set him back hard. I need to whap him with the stick. Sacrificing this movement will ensure the quality of the next five."

• Say "oops" and go on. Show-ring disasters happen. A paper bag blows through the ring. An umbrella opens. The footing is so horrible it scares your horse to death. He spooks at the flowers in the middle of your canter depart. So even though I never want you to accept a horrible canter depart in schooling, when you're test-riding (even for practice), I want you to learn to say, "OOPS! Horrible canter depart. I've got to go on," and quickly figure out how to make the next movement and the rest of the test brilliant.

• Keep your horse's attention, even at a crowded, chaotic showground. To learn to do that, "take your show on the road." Go to a

"Because most green horses shy at the judge's trailer, park a trailer where you can ride around it."

friend's barn. Show your horse strange sights, and figure out how they change him and what you need to do about it. Take him off by himself. Visit a show and make a point of getting him close to the competition arena. Look at the tents and trailers and other horses warming up. Walk around and graze.

Because most green horses shy at the judge's trailer, park a trailer where you can ride around it. (Ask Great-Aunt Gertie to sit inside for good measure.) Walk your horse by it, let him look at it, turn back and forth in front of it. Ride straight toward it in your test; if he's still backed off, don't make a point of getting all the way to C. Let him cut the corner; then, gradually, work him closer as you go. Hang banners, put coolers over the rail, set up a beach umbrella, play loud rock music. That's the real world. Gently help him learn to cope! And by the way . . .

• Learn to deal with it yourself! Don't complain to me that the warm-up ring is too crowded. That's probably the least obnoxious of the conditions you'll have to warm up under, so get out there and ride with a platoon of horses (otherwise *you're* the one who's going to be the menace in the warm-up). Warm up in a field. Warm up on a hillside. Or warm up as I've done—in a parking lot, weaving around trailers! Ride your test while a nutso horse is being longed. Ride in sand and on grass. Ride through puddles. Ride in mud. Ride when it's rainy, slippery, and wet. It ain't gonna hurt you. You ain't gonna melt. But you *are* gonna toughen up and be there with bells on.

• Don't freak out. What is it about "riding a test" that gets to your nerves? You probably don't have the option of learning to relax the way I learned (by riding fifty horses a day), so do the next best thing and ride with somebody watching. I don't necessarily mean the entire Mormon Tabernacle Choir. It can be Great-Aunt Gertie, who's double-

Defusing
Trailer Terrors

1. Courtney starts by giving Jester a chance to stand and look at the "judge's" trailer from the center line. He's obviously a little worried; she's rubbing his neck with her knuckles while keeping a soft feel of his mouth and a quiet leg on him, giving him confidence but not clutching or digging him with her spurs. (Putting both reins in one hand to pat with the other would leave her vulnerable if he startled; this light contact leaves her prepared whatever happens.) And "Great-Aunt Gertie"—Jean—is speaking to him. That's important: A lot of horses don't recognize that shape in the trailer as a human until it speaks!

2. Despite the confidence-building in photo 1, when they approach from the short side for the first time, Jester's decided this is a little more than he wants to deal with. Spotting Great-Aunt Gertie, he begins to spook, ready to wheel away. Courtney is sitting good and deep, a little behind the vertical, in the "driver's seat"; that will help keep her stable. (In fact, just looking at her upper body, you wouldn't know anything's going on.). Her lower leg's come up, which isn't ideal, but it *is* hanging onto his side, saying, "You stay to the right" —just what we want. Her hands are very nice, still going forward with him; she hasn't grabbed hard at his mouth. In a shy, you want to continue to use your hands as aids, not hang on with them, because the solution is to go forward. If you grab hold, you're taking away the use of the bit—because you've just made your horse dead in his mouth.

3. Now Jester's obviously trying to shy—his head is way up in the air. But Courtney's kept a straight line with his mouth, not pulling up or down; she's got her left leg on him and she's bending him strongly to the left, trying to leg-yield him toward that monster. It may not be elegant, but she isn't letting him run off with her: He's bent left, he's on the track; he's way above the bit, but she's controlling his placement, sitting deep, with her leg deep. (Ideally, I'd like her upper body back a little more to get her weight *really* down; the minute you start to get forward, you're vulnerable.)

4. Next time around (on next page), Jester's hard-pricked ears say he's still worried—but he's paying attention to Courtney and she's riding

DEFUSING TRAILER TERRORS *(continued)*

defensively, controlling every part of his body. She put him in a good bend in the previous corner, and she's keeping that bend here, making him look way to the inside, her left leg on him in leg-yield position. (The amount of leg depends on the horse. You may need to stop and leg-yield a step from the halt. But if you do halt, and you're getting into a situation where you think he may rear, give your hands forward, tell him to go forward, and don't hesitate to get someone on the ground or another horse to lead him past what's scaring him—or get off and lead him yourself a few times. As show-jumping great George Morris says, "You've got to have more time than the horse has." I had one horse so timid that I had to put a bucket of grain on the trailer ramp, then let him go up and take a little mouthful each time we went by—but getting him to go up for that first mouthful took a long time. The horse has to reach the point where he goes by because he's comfortable doing so, not because he's more afraid of you than of the trailer.) Courtney's worked through the problem enough that she's in a nice energetic trot with that left bend and a little outside rein. If Jester were very disobedient, she'd need her left rein to control the bend, her right rein encouraging his shoulders to stay right, and her left leg asking as if in a leg-yield. Here, I'd just like to see her lift her collapsed chest, square her rounded shoulders, and give herself the use of all her back as well as of both hands and legs.

5. There are moments, as we've just seen, where you must have your horse strongly on every aid. But one of the greatest mistakes you can make with a horse that's tight or high or fresh or nervous is to hold him there. That tension must have an escape route; otherwise, he'll get claustrophobic and the tension will build on itself. So here, having gone past the trailer monster under mega-control, Courtney has now offered Jester her aids: Her hands are forward, her legs are quiet, and she's allowing him to recover a little and just trot, giving him what I call "a chance to breathe." Just as you learn, in competition, to take that deep breath and let the tension out, you have to learn to let your horse do the same.

checking the test booklet to make sure you stay on course (but not calling the test, because you're riding it from memory, right?). It can be your family, your book-discussion group, or your fellow riders. And when you start to fall apart because now it's formal—somebody's watching you ride a test—ask yourself, "What am I afraid of? Why am I so worried about them watching me? And even if I make a complete fool of myself, are they going to remember tomorrow?"

If you've worked through the two dozen lessons before this one and practiced your test enough, you *know* your horse and what he'll do in different situations during the test. You're prepared to be there, and you're going to do the best you can. And if it's not good enough for the mailman, your fellow students, Great-Aunt Gertie, and whoever that other guy is standing over there, that's *their* problem, not yours. You're doing this for *you*, you're doing the best you can, and you will get up tomorrow and brush your teeth as you've always done. So enjoy! ■

LESSON 26

Show Day!

THERE'S A LOCAL ONE-DAY SHOW. You and your horse are going to début at Training Level. Are you ready?

I've taught you about riding a test. You've taken your horse to a friend's barn to see how he behaves away from home. You've developed a solid warm-up routine. And you've got peace of mind that comes from knowing all your gear is clean, repaired, and organized.

What's left? Learning how to compete.

So, in this lesson, I'll share some tips with you on . . .

- getting show smarts without showing
- showground details that make a big difference
- counting down your day
- staying focused and effective during your warm-up
- maximizing the moments before (and the sixty seconds after) the bell
- keeping your cool if you flub up

A DAY AT THE SHOW

Meet L.A. Baltic Sunstorm, a five-year-old Swedish Warmblood. He's not a horse I need to longe every day to get the bucks out, but he's a very intense horse, and he's going to his first show today. I don't expect him to be too bad, but I do want to give him a chance to get settled (something, you'll see, that he obviously needs!).

1. Our test is at 8:00 AM, but here, a little after 6:30, we're already at the showgrounds, Sunstorm's fully tacked up, and all I have to do to be presentable is take off this splendid skirt (which completely covers my white breeches) and switch coats. We left home at 4:00 AM so I'd have plenty of time to do what I'm starting off to do now: lead him around, let him see the judge's stand and all the other strange things, and longe him, getting him as relaxed as he can be before the crowds come and the show starts.

2. Starting out on the longe, Sunstorm is horrendous, but I'm not unhappy that he's bucking. I want him to let off some steam and get the kinks out. I have him out on a big circle, giving him as much space as I can; the long side reins just prevent him from getting totally out of control. Note, please, that we're completely by ourselves; this is not something to do where other people are trying to warm up—one reason I made sure to get here early. I wanted to be able to longe him here, which (though you may not be able to tell) is right behind the judge's stand, an area I want to accustom him to being in. (One flaw: He's not wearing boots. Failing to protect his legs with boots is a chance I don't usually take.)

3. After fifteen minutes or so on the longe, we took a break to get comfortable in the warm-up ring while it was still empty. Now we're walking slowly around the arena itself. Sunstorm is blowing his nose, obviously afraid of this letter; I'll let him stand here until he stops paying attention to it. Many people don't realize that letters—particularly tall ones—can scare horses, so they don't include them when they're doing this sort of walk. My horses are used to low-to-the-ground letters at home—but make the letters taller, or put flowers around them, and it's a whole different thing!

4. Back in our all-to-ourselves longeing spot behind the judge's stand, about half an hour after we started, he's in a nice rhythmic trot and stretching down toward those side reins, so we can stop.

5. At the judge's stand—which we can check out like this because we got here way before the show started—Sunstorm is again a little bit off the deep end, and I'm looking at his eye and being careful where I place myself in relation to him. This is VERY important: Whenever you're handling any horse, watch his eyes and ears; they'll tell you where his attention is and where he's headed. Don't make the common mistake of talking to your friends or looking around; to be safe, you've GOT to pay attention to (number one) his eyes and (number two) his ears. Sunstorm is both looking at the judge's stand and looking for an escape route; that's why my hand's on his chest. I've got the longe line in two hands, as well; if he does something

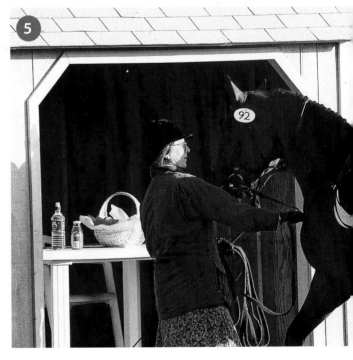

- making a graceful exit
- and warming up for your next class!

Advance Preparation

Go to a dressage show and watch with the purpose of understanding how the show runs. Better yet, volunteer—preferably as a steward in the warm-up area, so you get a feel for how people deal with nerves and commotion, and for what happens when somebody's ready too soon or not ready on time.

Get the lay of the land. If you've never been to the facility where you'll be showing, call the show secretary. Find out how far from the arena you'll be parking. Where's the show office? Do you need to bring water for your horse? Is there shade? Is there a proper longeing area? How's the footing? Do you need studs for grass, or pads for rock-hard ground?

Calculate a countdown. The show secretary tells you that your first test is at 10:15 AM. Work back from there. If you plan a forty-five-minute warm-up (and it should be no longer), that's 9:30. If you'll need ten minutes to get to the warm-up area, that's 9:20. Ten minutes to tack up, that's 9:10. Twenty minutes to groom, ten minutes to get yourself ready, ten minutes to sign in, ten minutes to park, thirty minutes to drive to the show, ten minutes to load . . . Add on an hour for walking around and chilling—and, because your horse may balk, you may get lost, or you may have to longe, an hour to spare. Bottom line: Load at about 5:30 AM.

When You Arrive

Park as close to the action as possible (unless your horse is so green that he's better without the crowds wandering by). Leave enough room to work around him safely, and enough that you don't crowd or block anybody else.

Sign in. Pick up your number (and, as soon as you can, attach it to your bridle, saddle pad, or halter, so you know where it is). Check the program to make sure you're in the classes you signed up for and you ride when you think you do (the times may have changed).

Check the clock with the show secretary. Is the show running on time, or is everything an hour late because the judge was delayed?

Find your rings and the warm-up areas. How close are they to each other? How busy? Will you need to start in a quieter warm-up, then finish where it's more crowded? Or can you jump right in?

Watch a test in your ring if the show's already started. Where are the puddles? Where are the deep spots? Is the horse shying at anything? Where and how do you enter? Is there only a right- or left-hand turn? (Some rings are set up that way.) And is the turn easy or tight?

Write down the numbers you need to know on a "cheat sheet" you'll keep in your pocket (so you don't have to count on anybody else): the time you're due in the ring, the number of your class, the test you're riding, the ring number, the bridle numbers of the three horses ahead of you (I'll explain why), when you have to get your horse ready, and when to get on.

Now deal with your horse. Unload him, walk him around, and let him hang out and graze. Go around the warm-up area (without getting in the way). If the show hasn't started, walk him outside your ring for a good look inside the trailer or the judge's booth, the tents, and the bleachers. Groom him up a bit; if there's time, let him graze some more, or put him in the trailer to relax and eat. Get yourself ready, and then tack up. (I always try to warm up with everything as I'll want it when I'm going

dramatic and he gets away from my right hand, I'll still have him with my left hand.

I don't have a tight rein; I'm not holding Sunstorm right up by the bit. This way I'm able to keep a little distance and use my hand both to calm him a little and to push on him so he doesn't run over me. But I'm not making him stand still; I'm letting him walk in a little circle because he really is very afraid. I'm not forcing anything: I want to give him enough time to get comfortable with the judge's stand because he learns there's nothing to be afraid of here—and I don't want him more afraid of me than of the judge's stand. And we don't just go by the booth; I let him look IN so he knows there's nothing scary inside. It's one thing to walk by something; it's another to be appearing to walk into it—as he'll feel he is when he comes down the center line.

6. Warm-up time—and (next page) obviously a complete out-of-control moment as Sunstorm wheels away from some jump standards outside the ring. Yes, he caught me off guard, but I'm not panicked; it's "OK, here we are, he's leaping to the side, I'm staying on," not "Oh, my God!" By the time his

Show Day!

A DAY AT THE SHOW
(continued)

front feet get on the ground again, I intend to be reconnected with his mouth, have him back under control—and move on . . .

7. . . . as we've done here. Sunstorm's expression is still a bit worried, but we've quickly come back together. My purpose here isn't to school him; we did that at home. It's to get his attention so that I can help him gain confidence, and to give him enough time to get used to everything. Sunstorm is a very attentive horse: His nostrils are flared, and he's obviously not relaxed—but he's on my aids, working with me, and allowing me to give him confidence.

8. Time for our test: The first thing I need to do is get Sunstorm very relaxed and confident; so, having gone around the ring once, I've quietly halted to help settle him. I have a tight horse but one who is looking to me to help him, to direct him, to give him confidence. In my first test on this horse, my entire goal is to get him in there and let him find out that neither the judge's stand nor the letters nor anything else is going to eat him. Whatever happens above that is a plus. (I also hope I won't humiliate myself—but if I do, it won't be the first or last time!)

9. I want to give Sunstorm more time around the judge's box; so here, at the A end, I'm turning him quietly around to head back there, doing a sort of turn on the haunches to get his attention very much to me. Instead of wasting time going on around the arena, I'm concentrating on the areas that worry him most.

10. And here's our goal. Sunstorm's trotting pleasantly, on the aids, attentive, and on the track, passing the horrendously terrifying judge's stand that he wouldn't even be led up to early this morning. The confidence he's showing and the way he's "got it all together" never would have happened without the large amount of time I spent preparing. (By the way, he won both of his classes at this show and finished the day as Training Level Champion!)

into the ring—coat on, hat on, no bandages.)

When You Get to the Warm-Up

. . . look for the three people who ride before you. If you don't see one of them, check with the in-gate official to see if the competitor has scratched, and make a mental note that maybe you can go early if ready. If you see all three of them still there long after they should have been doing their tests, figure that the show is running late. Also keep an eye on the ring where you'll be competing; it's a way to reinforce your test ("Yep, she did pick up the canter at A") and to keep tabs on ring conditions. Is the puddle drying out? Is the deep spot getting deeper? Is the lady in the armchair at K still spooking the horses?

Now, remember . . .

Warm-Up Isn't Kamikaze Time

There's nothing worse or more dangerous than a bunch of people who don't know how to share a warm-up because they're inexperienced, they don't look up, they're unpredictable, or they're just too self-absorbed. Riding in the warm-up area needs to be a team effort and to follow *universal rules of conduct*:

- Look up and ahead.
- Always pass oncoming riders left side to left side.
- Yield to any rider doing a more difficult movement.
- Wait your turn (don't start across the diagonal when somebody's there doing a canter pirouette).
- Don't stand on the rail gossiping with friends or adjusting your coat.
- Don't stand in the middle with three people taking off bandages.
- Don't monopolize half the area tak-

ing a lesson. (If you need a lesson, you're not ready to show!)

You're not here to school; you're here to warm up, and this you know how to do: Put your horse on the aids at the walk and get him bending, moving forward, halting, and listening. (The more walk work you can do *outside* the warm-up area, by the way, the better—he'll get another look-see, and you'll be out of everybody's way.) Then, unless the canter is his best warm-up gait, trot on passive contact with many changes of direction, some trot/walk transitions, even figures from your test—corners, diagonals, 20-meter circles, center lines, transitions at the letters (or at that dandelion or at the lady with the ugly hat). Unless he's super, super hyper (and he may be), he should be in a nice working trot in a few minutes. Have a nice big left and right canter to make sure the kinks are out. Then walk, tally the results, and . . .

Decide What You've Got to Do

Is your horse tough to bend left? Is he sucking back in the canter departs? Is he ignoring your whoas? If his trot feels great, leave it alone. If he flings his head every time you pick up the canter, keep him a little low during walk/trot transitions. Then go on a 20-meter trot circle and try to get everything right in the canter transition—on the aids, listening, balanced, and feeling good. If his head still comes up, do more suppling at the trot, get him deeper, shorten and lengthen, and then try the canter again.

A general rule of thumb: If things are getting better, give him a breather. If things are getting worse, do something else.

If He's a Basket Case . . .

. . . think of those cold, windy days at home when you hadn't ridden him for three days, and do whatever settled him then: longeing

STAYING ORGANIZED

1. This side of my show bag houses an extra pair of everything—gloves, breeches, shirt stock, underwear, socks—as well as makeup, bobby pins and safety pins, sewing kit, extra buttons, hairnets, mirror, Band-Aids®. (My coat is in the other side.) Right after the show, I put back or replace anything I've used, so it's all ready for next time.

2. Easily visible inside the lid of my rolling tack box is my time sheet, telling me when I'm supposed to do what throughout the day. (The see-through show-bag pockets are another good place for a time sheet.) The numbers belong to horses that have finished showing; they're ready to be turned

(as long as you can longe him safely), sitting on his back with somebody leading or walking beside you, galloping in a half-seat, letting him trot with his head straight up in the air, or going deep and doing transitions. If things are *really* falling apart, use your common sense. Is the ring just too busy to deal with? Find a quieter place. Above all, do not get your horse into a tizzy. If he won't stand because he's nervous, the last thing you want to do is say, "Stand, you jerk!" and go KICK, WHAP as he gets more frantic. Instead, relax him by loosening your rein and patting him—or acknowledge that

this time it just ain't gonna work, so once you're in the ring, you'll have to salute fast and get on with it.

From Warm-Up to Ring

Whoops! You allotted forty-five minutes to your warm-up, but after twenty minutes you're ready. What to do? Take a fifteen-minute walk; then come back and warm up for ten more minutes before your test.

Need to take off boots or bandages, or put your coat on? Same thing: Do it ten minutes before your ride time, so you're warming up until the moment you're ready to go.

And when, exactly, is that? Well, if you've been keeping an eye on the rider ahead of you, you know when she started her test, right? Leave the warm-up and head for the ring as soon as she begins her walk work and you'll be right on time: neither too late (so you rush or miss the bell) nor too early (so you have to stand around or walk on a loose rein—especially bad if your horse takes that to mean he's done, so he gets resistant or even belligerent when you try to put him back together).

As soon as the rider ahead of you salutes, get right in there around the ring and use every second you have to figure out if you can just trot both ways around the ring and provide your guy a horse's-eye view of everything (the letters, the judge, the flags in the distance . . .), throw in some halts, and tune him to your leg and hand.

What if you get "Eeek! It's a trailer!"? Just walk back and forth in front of it until the judge rings the bell—but even as you do, in your fuzzy little brain you should already be planning two movements ahead: "OK, I enter on the right hand at A because that's the way I get my straightest halt, I track right at C, circle at B, then do the diagonal," and so on.

Ask Not for Whom the Bell Rings . . .

. . . and don't stop breathing, start hanging on the reins, or decide the bell is a starting gun. Sixty seconds is plenty of time to trot all the way around the ring (try it at home a few times). Even if you're at C, you'll get to A comfortably if you trot down the long side, establish gait and tempo and frame and balance, maybe even do one last trot/halt/trot transition, make a big loop, and then enter.

Now, repeat after me: "My job is done. I am here to show what I have done before. There is nothing for me to worry about now, and there is nothing I can fix." Prepared or not, do the best you can. Have a good time and show off your horse. If things fall apart, it won't be the first time. If you go off course and the judge rings the bell, stop and make sure you know what your mistake was and where he wants you to pick up again. You've lost only two points (and there's no way on earth you're going to get them back), so just make the rest of the test that much better.

After Your Final Salute . . .

. . . let your horse have the reins, and— unless the judge indicates he wants to speak to you—free-walk forward for two or three strides, make a big comfortable turn, head toward A, and leave, because it's over. As a courtesy to the judge, the management, and the remaining competitors, get out as quickly as you can, and go away—so you don't block the entrance or cause a distraction when Great-Aunt Gertie bawls about what a star you were (or you bawl about what a disaster it was). If you need to, return to the warm-up area for a brief and quiet little schooling moment, but not a major session. That's homework.

Before Your Next Test

Watch your ride if you had it taped, and try to read the comments from your first test. Even if you'll be riding in front of a different judge, you can still learn: "Gee, I didn't realize he was 'halting haunches-right.' Maybe I can fix that." Or "Hmmm, 'not forward enough.' Maybe I *never* ride forward enough." Hey! You just got your money's worth! Take a chance on being too forward in your next test!

And that may come up very soon if it's a small show, so get right back into the warm-up area. If it's a big show, you may have to put your horse up for two hours. In either case, you've already worked him. Get the two of you settled, tune him up for five or ten minutes, and you're ready.

Go for It!

Competing is one of those activities that requires experience. Only in the show ring can you figure out how best to showcase your horse, how to recover from your mistakes, how to hide your faults, and how to deal with nerves (yours and his). It's where you demonstrate what you've prepared and find out what you haven't prepared quite as well as you thought. Competing—it's challenging and fun and, above all, a wonderful learning experience. Get your money's worth. ■

back in. (First thing after picking up your number, put it on your bridle; that's the one thing everyone forgets.)

3. How did you do? Pick up the score sheet from your first test—as my student Elvira Michelich has done here—as soon as it's available, giving you (and your trainer, if you have a trainer with you) a chance to talk about it and maybe figure out if there's anything you can improve on in your next class: not long-term schooling problems, but things like circles that weren't quite big enough, or a whole test being a little too slow or a little too fast.

FOUR DIFFERENT FRAMES FOR TRAINING LEVEL

To help you develop a feel for acceptable Training Level ways of going—and for what is *really* correct, whether the judging reflects it or not—let's look at four quite different Training Level horses from my barn, all at the same moment in the trot: when the weight is on the left front leg in the forward phase of the stride. After we've looked at each, I'll place them as if I were judging them in a class—so have some fun and do the same as we go along.

1A. Four-year-old Joseph, a Thoroughbred and a very pleasant, basic Training Level horse, looks relaxed here, accepting the bit nicely with soft flexion. By nature he's a little on his forehand—hind legs somewhat out behind him, not shifting his God-given balance back. But as soon as he comes off his forehand, he won't be a Training Level horse any more. The only correct way to change his balance is by his learning to shift his weight during transitions, going up and down hills, and maybe jumping some fences—not by a rider's pulling and kicking.

1B. Here's the proof. When Courtney tried for the picture she

After the Show: Be Your Own Trainer!

OK—YOU'VE GONE TO YOUR FIRST show. You may have had an absolute ball— but from what I know of life and dressage, more likely you had some good, some bad, and some ugly.

Now that the show's over, you have a choice. You can go on being a student—a dabbler—who packs away her ribbons, tests, videos, and memories, and learns nothing from them. Or you can start to *become your own trainer* by using the show as a valuable learning experience. By figuring out why things did and didn't go well, not only can you reassess and regroup your training program, but you can improve your schooling at home and make your show experience that much better next time.

If, as I'm guessing, what you want to do is learn, this last lesson will help you with your "post-game analysis" by giving you lots of tips on . . .

• getting the most out of your test scores and comments (including a numerical system to keep track of exactly how you're doing—see "Chart Your Progress" on page 172)

• learning from your disasters by regrouping and developing coping strategies

• deciding whether you jumped the gun and need more lessons and/or schooling time at home, and

• tipping the balance in your and your horse's favor at the next show.

Let's start by making use of those most valuable learning tools that come from dressage showing. Let's . . .

Look at Your Tests

Read the judge's comments in the context of your work.

Take some comments with a grain of salt. The judge can only judge what he sees. Where a comment is critical, was he seeing a glitch you need to address now or a glitch that's covered by a long-term objective you're working toward?

Say your horse has always been a fussbudget at the halt but he just happened to stand still at the show. The judge said, "Halt not square." Yeah, he's right—but *you're* just thrilled that your horse stood. You'd be a fool to let the judge's comment force you to do something you're not ready for, like fussing at your horse to be absolutely square and losing the immobility you just got hold of. Forget square. Your halt will be square in a few months. Right now, you're working on quiet.

Or say your horse goes long and low-ish with his nose poked out a little. He accepts the bit, but he isn't truly 100 percent on the aids. The judge writes, "The horse must be more through and on the bit." Have confidence in knowing enough about yourself, your horse, and your training program to say, "Yeah, that's true, but we're not quite there yet. I'm being penalized for something that really isn't wrong for my horse's progress at this particular time. I'm not going to worry about it."

thought the judge would want—putting Joe more together and shifting his weight back—all she did was pull his head in, shorten his stride, and destroy the qualities she had. This horse just isn't ready to carry himself in that frame yet. The tightness in her arm shows how much she's holding him together; that shortened stride is an even bigger giveaway. Ultimately Joe's frame will shorten because he learns to step deeper and carry more weight behind, so he's able to lift his shoulders and neck— not because he flexes more!

2A. Another four-year-old (next page), Lambada, a Dutch Warmblood, is built with his neck up a bit higher and steps underneath a little more, giving him better engagement and greater freedom in the shoulder. But he's still obviously very much a Training Level horse—and Marjaleena is riding him within his abilities. Yes, he's going to beat Joe

FOUR DIFFERENT FRAMES FOR TRAINING LEVEL
(continued)

here—because he's naturally better balanced. But trying to make Joe into another Lambada right now would be a mistake. Joe's going to be good; he just needs more time.

2B. Looking at this photo and 2A shows the importance of comparing the same moment in the stride: This photo shows a split-second earlier in the trot stride, where Lambada looks much less on his front end. It's the same horse, doing the same thing, but a different look.

3. Your first reaction to Wellington, an eight-year-old German-bred, may well be "How nice." He looks much more advanced than our first two horses: nice sense of energy, frame up in front, head on the vertical. But look closely and you'll see that he's very tight throughout his body—particularly in his shoulders, neck, and head—and isn't tracking under well at all. Where Lambada's hind foot stepped just about in the print of his front foot, Willie's two prints are a good distance

Take other comments to heart. Which comments? The ones that apply no matter where your horse is in his training. Examples: "horse not forward enough"; "more bend to the left"; "circles shaped like eggs, needs to be more accurate"; "rider tends

to sit to left." And if you ever get "horse not prepared for transitions," OUCH! That's a knock on the head about a basic building block that you really need to attend to.

Remember, there's no accounting for tastes. It happens all the time. You ride a shaky Test 1 and score 56 percent. Then you ride a much better Test 2 under another judge and score 54 percent. Which is why, even though you do want to pay attention to scores and ribbons and placings—they're why you're showing—you don't want to let them run your life.

Say your horse is a little on the forehand and not totally on the bit, but he's soft and quiet and you ride a very fluid, pleasant, easy test. Another horse is tight, tense,

and a little abrupt, but his face is on the vertical and he's dead accurate. Except for the accuracy, that's not the way you want *your* horse to go; but if that's the performance this particular judge wants to see, you're going to get beaten. Don't let that make

you change what you know is right.

Disaster Management

Think of what went wrong at this show and how you can make it go right in the next one.

Reevaluate your countdown. OK. You had some disasters. You were totally disrupted when another horse bucked his rider off in the warm-up ring. Your stock tie came undone and flapped in the breeze. Your horse was a complete, raving maniac. Figure out now what you need to cope next time: A stock pin? A heck of a lot more time to get your guy settled? Should you have longed him? Did you need to get there earlier and let him acclimate when everything was really quiet? Or do you just need to expose him more by hauling him off to every little dog-and-pony show in the neighborhood?

Keep his attention. Did your horse refuse to go near the judge's trailer? Park a trailer in your ring at home. Did he keep shying at the flowers? Practice dealing with shying. (And accept that shying is part of showing and isn't going to go away, especially if yours is a looky kind of horse. World Champion and Olympic gold medalist Rembrandt never quit shying at the flowers around the ring—but his rider, Nicole

apart. Riding him with a slightly longer, lower neck would give him a little more freedom in his back and help him track under a little more.

4. Here's another "first glances can be deceiving" photo. Five-year-old Crystal Corynette, an Arabian, is very tense, and that affects her way of going. Yes, she's showing a nice trot, tracking under very well, but she's not showing the basics required at Training Level: relaxation, acceptance of the bit, basic self-carriage. She doesn't have Joe's stabilization; she wants to rush and is tight, especially in her neck, from being held back. I'm comfortable showing Joe, but I'm not showing Cory yet because she isn't stabilized—even though most people are going to like her picture a little better than his because she doesn't look quite so on the forehand.

OK, make your picks and turn the page to see how your choices compare with mine.

Uphoff, did a superb job of forging ahead in spite of it.)

Practice maintaining his obedience too, even when his mind momentarily zips off to the trailer or the flowerpot or the bucking horse, because there will *always* be something distracting. Flags flap. Horses clatter in and out of trailers. Children run through bleachers. Deer wander out of the bushes. (That happened at the show featured in Lesson 26's photos!) The bad news: Every show has its distractions. The good news: I've given you the tools to cope, if you'll just keep your head and use them: Get your horse a little too deep; bend him away from the monster and leg-yield toward it; ask for transitions, always transitions; or do any other exercise that gets his attention on you and reminds him that obedience comes first, even when there's a monster. Really, my friends, that's one of the fun things about showing: knowing that there *are* all these little unpredictable disruptions, taking them on as challenges, and getting through them by training your horse.

Never give up. If something totally fell apart—completely and totally—OK, it fell apart. You could have given up, which was going to get you absolutely zero nowhere, or you could have said, "All right. Boy, I've blown this. I practically fell off; I had to circle six times; I started riding the wrong test; and even with the judge coaching, I never got the right-lead canter. But I'm going to go on and get to the end of the test and make it the best I can under the circumstances." And you know what? It was a horrible test, and you got a horrible score, but it was also a lesson in recovering and going on. Giving up never makes things better. You are not the first or last person to have a horrendous ride.

Above all, remember that your horse wasn't out there saying, "Heh- heh, I'm going to show *her*. I'm going to humiliate her out here in front of everybody." That was *not* going on in his head. Now you have

Let's Pin the Class

The order I would pick is Lambada, Joe, Wellington, and Cory. Here's why:

- Lambada is the most athletic, scopey mover. Yes, he's a little on the forehand, but he's very relaxed, accepting the bridle in a lovely way and moving forward nicely.

- Joe doesn't have the scope of movement and isn't as light, but he's in the top two "correctnesswise." He and Lambada are both on track.

- Willie shows the best balance of all. But in reaching for that higher-level balance, he's lost the pure correctness of stride—the engagement and reach aren't there—and he shows the tightness that comes with that loss.

- Though Cory shows length of stride and is in an acceptable frame, that frame is tense and being held together. Unless I get her stabilized now, so that she can trot without being held back, this hole in her training will get me in trouble down the road. The same is true with Willie: Unless I get him to go with his back freer, perhaps riding him a little longer and lower, I may be able to have him do the tricks, but I'm never going to develop his gaits to the utmost. And that will catch me.

All of which leads me to say that I wish more judges wouldn't heavily penalize things that aren't serious in the long run. For example, comparing Cory and Joe, she may look prettier right now, but she's going to be in trouble if I let her tension continue. Joe may be the least athletic of the four now, but there's nothing wrong with what he's doing. We're smart not to mess with him—and we just have to hope that the judge sees the wisdom of "riding what you have" and not trying to make a horse into something he isn't.

to do some work in *your* head to figure out how to help him help you, so the two of you can go to the show, work together, and not be at cross-purposes.

To Show or Not to Show (Next Time)

I've said it before, and I'll say it again: You cannot become a good show rider without showing. However, I strongly believe that you should not continue showing at this time if any of the following statements describes you:

• You cannot put forth the caliber of performance at home that you want at the show.

• You perform exactly the way you perform at home and get a 45 percent. In my estimation, 60 percent means you're pretty OK, and 50 percent means that at least something's on the right track. Less than 50 percent is totally inadequate (unless your horse just happened to blow up and pull off a bunch of 2's in the midst of the 5's and 6's—I've had my share of 40 percents under those circumstances). If you scored consistently below 50 percent for all three tests—you look down the column and all you got were 4's—stay home and use your show-entry money to pay for lessons.

• You cannot ride your test from memory. (I can live with your wanting a reader for a boost of confidence, but not as the only way you'll get through the test.)

• You don't have the confidence to think for yourself, analyze things, do stuff on your own, and not be completely dependent on an instructor (especially if you turn into a puppet who can't even get into the arena without a full-on lesson—ooooh, don't monopolize my corner of the warm-up area doing that).

• You don't have the focus to go on when something falls apart. What is focus?

Being aware of your goal and not letting anything distract you from it. Being able to pick right up and continue, without wailing, "Oh, it's falling apart. Woe is me." Instantly cantering again when your horse breaks—not trotting around, reorganizing, getting frustrated, and walking. Regrouping and moving along when he shies—not clutching and making sixty-two circles. Sitting down in the saddle when he bucks—not stopping and whining or looking pleadingly at your instructor as if to say, "Why is he doing this to me? Come and make it right." That's focus—and it will make you your own "trainer," rather than a helpless student looking for support all the time.

Once More Unto the Breach, Dear Friends

So . . . when to show again? That depends. If you discovered a real hole in your schooling—for example, your horse just isn't accepting contact—fill it in first. If, when disaster struck, he got too much out of control for you to cope with by using the tools I've given you, do more work on basics. But if you were just tense and tight, or if your horse was just overwhelmed by the commotion, get out there and keep going down the road until showing is old hat.

When you do go showing, though, remember that it's not a perfect world. Don't show where the footing's bad. Don't show if the atmosphere is excessively disruptive, especially if your horse tends to get a little overwrought. And always go with a positive attitude and with a goal, be it doing at least *some* of your canter departs, staying unrattled, or getting him past the trailer.

Bottom line: Don't *just* go out and show again. Go out and show again with an understanding of what you've learned from last time and what you're going to do to make this show better. *That's* being your own trainer!

Chart Your Progress

Start a show notebook, systematically compare your scores, and you'll quickly get a picture of what needs work, what's falling apart, what's improving, and what's just dandy the way it is.

This info is important for several reasons—especially because most of us tend to drill what's already good and avoid the stuff that takes work. If you see down in black and white that you always get a good mark on your center line and halt, you know it's OK. If your marks are always low, however, you can take note and do something about it.

Here's how to chart your progress. List all your test movements on the left-hand side of a page. (Training Level has some twenty-odd movements altogether. Not every movement appears in every test, and the movements rarely occur in the same order, but you can still compare a walk-trot transition with a walk-trot transition whenever and wherever it occurs.) Rule some columns across the page. Pick a "base score"—the numerical score you'll be happy to receive on each movement. Let's say that for now it's 6 (which, if you get it on every movement, will give you a very presentable 60 percent on your tests).

With test sheets in hand, fill in one column per test, per show. At the top, note the test, date, the judge (if you want to keep track of that), and your percentage score. Going down the column, compare your scores with your base score. If you got a 7 on the entrance and halt in your first test, for example, put down a +1. If you got a 4, put a -2.

By the time you've charted your first three tests, a pattern will emerge that gives shape to what you need to concentrate on. For example, if your 20-meter trot circles to the left scored +1, +2, and +1, but the ones to the right scored -2, -1, and -1, which 20-meter trot circles do you need to work on? ■

Training Level	T-1 7/5	T-2 7/5	T-3 8/8	T-4 8/8
Enter, halt, salute	-1	-1	0	-1
Trot ○ left 20m	+2	0	+1	——
Canter L	-2	-1	-2	-2
Canter ○ L 20m	0	0	0	0
Canter L—trot	-1	0	-1	0
Trot—med. walk	+1	+1	+2	+2
Free walk—med. walk	+1	0	+2	+1
Walk—trot	0	0	+1	+1
Trot ○ R 20m	0	0	0	——
Canter R	-2	-2	-1	0
Canter ○ R 20m	——	——	——	——
Canter R—trot	——	——	——	——
Center line, halt, salute	——	——	——	——
B turn L (T) E turn R	——	——	——	——
B turn R (T) E turn L	——	——	——	——
Change rein (T) diag.	——	——	——	——
Chewing reins	——	——	——	——
T ○ L @ X	——	——	——	——
T ○ R @ X	——	——	——	——
FXM loop	——	——	——	——
KXH loop	——	——	——	——

T = Trot   C = Canter   ○= Circle   L = Left   R = Right

Show-Preparation Countdown

COMPETING MEANS MORE THAN simply riding a test. You want to enter at A feeling calm, confident, and focused, knowing you're as prepared as you can possibly be. To help you do that, I've put together a monthly countdown of what you'll need to do, starting five months before your show date. It'll guide you through the nitty-gritty details—from setting goals and reviewing tests to checking equipment and lining up transportation—that make for a successful show day.

Five Months Out: Set Your Goals

Believe it or not, identifying your goals is an important first step in show preparation.

• Decide *why* you want to show. To win awards? To have fun? Or (my first choice) to test your progress? If climbing the ladder of training is your main focus, you'll want to be aware that it is very difficult to school more advanced work than you're showing without occasionally worrying your horse or messing up your test movements.

• Get copies of the tests from local tack stores, through catalogues, or directly from USA Equestrian (phone: 859-258-2472; e-mail: information@equestrian.org; Web site: www.equestrian.org).

• Decide what level and what tests you want to ride. How? By understanding that dressage tests are not to demonstrate what you're working on now or to forecast what you hope to accomplish someday, but to showcase the movements, gaits, and transitions that are easy *now* for you and your horse. Here's a general guideline:

Following the program I've laid out in this book, you should be able to do the walk, rising and sitting trot, and canter, plus the transitions—within and between gaits—called for at Training Level.

• Map out your show schedule. Decide how many shows you want to go to and when. If your horse is older and settled, spread them out a bit; if he's new or green, get mileage by going to two or three in a row. If your pocketbook's thin, focus on one-day shows; three classes give you plenty of opportunity to achieve your goal. Check for shows with good footing, good warm-up, and—if you do stay over—good stabling.

• Memorize your tests—you cannot ride your best unless you do. Use memory tricks: Think of designs and patterns, rather than just letters; for example, remember that through Third Level, all odd-numbered tests make the turn at C to the left and even-numbered tests make it to the right. Lay letters on the rug and walk, trot, and canter around the living room. Make a cassette tape of the tests, complete with pauses before the movements so you can say them as they come up. Silently call the movements as you watch others ride the tests. Above all, DON'T tell me you don't have enough time to learn them!

Four Months Out: Get Your Stuff in Order

• Check your clothes for fit and comfort. (Both, believe me, are critical to riding a good test.) Get a looser coat or a tighter hunt cap if you need to. Find your gloves. Retrieve your stock pin from the jewelry box. Get your boots stretched, or have them reheeled or resoled, if they need it. If they're new, break them in, because nothing is worse than brand-new boots on show day.

• Set up a horse-show clothes bag—the kind with nifty compartments for storing all your clean show clothes: coat, breeches (including spares in case of disaster), belt, shirt, underwear, stock tie, stock pin, earrings, makeup if you use it, hairnets, bobby pins, safety pins, rubber bands, BandAids®, two pairs of gloves—so clothes can safely be the last thing on your mind the night before the show. (I can walk into my closet on a moment's notice, grab my show bag, and go.)

• Check your tack. Carefully examine all buckles and all stitching. Make sure everything fits, is legal for showing (check the USA Eq Rule Book), and is in good repair. If not, now's the time to fix it.

• Get your technique down. Learn now how to polish your boots, put your hair in a bun, tie a stock tie (and don't tell me you can't, because anybody can—just ask a friend to show you, or read the instructions in the package), and braid your horse's mane.

• Make sure your trailer is in good shape.

Three Months Out: How's It Going?

• Start practicing several test movements in a row, instead of just doing movements separately—so that you begin to see, for example, the difference between a halt, a halt on the center line, and a halt on the center line after you've done your canter work and your horse is a little strong, heavy, dull, or bored.

• Experiment. When you enter at A and come up the center line, do you get better, straighter halts off a left turn or off a right turn? Knowing that may make a big differ-

ence when you get to the show.

• Ask yourself, "What is and isn't working?" If, despite following these lessons conscientiously, you're still struggling with a basic problem—your horse remains very stiff to the left, say, or he continually goes splat in his canter-trot transitions—it may be time to get a lesson or two.

• Figure out how much time you need to warm up, and what exercises you need to ride, to have your horse working at his best. Establish how much get-ready time he needs, under normal circumstances, to show off his best self—for some horses, it's ten minutes; for others, an hour. If he becomes more tense as you work, ride early, put him away, and bring him back out just before you go into the arena. The mistake most people make is to leave their best work in the warm-up ring. They wear their horses out by drilling—either things they can do, or things they can't (which just frustrates them). Don't be one of those "most people." Practice at home!

Two Months Out: Test Yourself Before You Ride the Test

Take the time now, with two months still to go before you show, to make absolutely sure all your skills and bits and pieces are working. Every ride, as you ride, run through the following checklist of questions. (Hint: I want to hear a resounding "yes" to each and every one!)

• Can you come to a walk within four strides of a canter-trot transition?

• Can you go from sitting to posting to sitting to posting without making your horse's trot tempo, frame, self-carriage, and length of stride change?

• Can you shorten stride trotting down center line without your horse taking over and breaking to the walk?

• Are you including a straight line every time you ride a short side? (If your short

> "The mistake most people make is to leave their best work in the warm-up ring."

sides are like parts of 20-meter circles, you've got to fix them.)

• On a circle, can you give up the inside rein for a few strides and not have your horse lose the bend?

• Are you showing a touch more bend on circles and corners than you are on straight lines?

• When you pick up the canter in the corner, are you solidly on the track next to the first letter on the long side, and not somewhere out in the middle of nowhere?

• When you gather up the reins to go from free to medium walk, does your horse stay completely relaxed and not anticipate the transition to trot?

• Are you showing an equal amount of bend in either direction on the circle?

• Is your horse looking very slightly to the inside (and never to the outside) on the long sides of the arena?

• Are you leading your horse with your eyes and not staring at his mane?

• Can you do any and all figures, transitions, and movements under less-than-perfect conditions and on any surface you may encounter, be it sand, grass, or even puddles?

One Month Out: Dress Rehearsal!

• Make sure your tests are reeeally memorized—and by "reeeally," I mean you can recite them straight through without pausing, pick up at any movement and know exactly where you are, what you're doing, and where you're going, and sit in your living room and visualize yourself actually coming down the center line, knowing you have to ride that little half-halt, get him off your right rein, and give him a little poke with your left spur.

• Take your show on the road and find out how much time—away from home—you need to warm up so you're neither late nor so early that you're sitting on your horse for

hours and wearing him out. (If you truly know your horse, once you've competed a little, you should be able to time your warm-up to the minute.) Give yourself a little more time for him to adjust—time you can take up in hand-walking. See if trailering itself makes him a little stiff and tight; if it does, make a note that he'll need a little extra suppling after a trailer ride. Find out if he becomes a screaming idiot when you separate him from his barn buddy on the trailer (and make a note to organize separate trailers, or stabling on opposite ends of the show grounds).

Checklist for the Big Day

• Find the warm-up ring and the arena you'll be riding in—and make sure you know how to get from one to the other.

• Survey the arena for indentations, deep footing, slippery spots, puddles, and distractions, so you can anticipate and maybe avoid problems. (Watching other rides will also tell you about footing and potential distractions.)

• Sit at A or C (or however you picture yourself riding in that arena) and visualize yourself riding the perfect test.

• Nervous? Tell anybody who upsets you—your mother, your husband, your best friend—to stay away. Instead of getting discouraged and starting to believe you don't belong in the warm-up because an Olympic-level rider is in there on some fabulous horse, take inspiration from that rider. Forget about people watching you. The other riders are concentrating on their own stuff; and as for the general public—if your horse has his tail and his head straight up in the air, they're probably thinking, "Wow! Look at that one. He's really prancing." Finally . . . shut up!!! We don't want—and you don't need—to hear that you don't think you're ready, you couldn't get the left-lead canter depart this morning, your horse is hyper, or you're sooo scared. All you're doing is building up your nerves and getting on ours. ■